Walking With the Saints

FINDING ANAM CARA AND MODERN HEALING
IN THE CELTIC TRADITION

BOOK THREE

"I was like a stone lying in the deep mud; and He that is mighty came, and in His mercy lifted me up."

Stuart McGhie

Copyright © 2026 Stuart McGhie

All rights reserved. This book or any portion thereof may not be reproduced or used in any manner whatsoever without the express written permission of the publisher, except for the use of brief quotations in a book review.

ISBN (Paperback) 979-8-90243-302-6

Contents

Introduction:	3
Chapter 1: The Communion of Saints	16
Chapter 2: The Saints: Who They Are and Why They Matter	28
Chapter 3: The Theology of Spiritual Companionship	40
Chapter 4: Prayer and Invocation: Speaking With the Saints	53
Chapter 5: Fasting and Prayer: Intensifying Your Spiritual Practice	67
Chapter 6: Meditation and Contemplation: Encountering the Saints	80
Chapter 7: Devotional Practices: Honouring the Saints in Daily Life	92
Chapter 8: Living in Communion: Daily, Weekly and Seasonal Rhythms	105
Chapter 9: St Patrick: The Courage of the Captive	118
Chapter 10: St Brigid: The Generosity of the Flame	131
Chapter 11: St Columba: The Warrior Poet's Transformation	143
Chapter 12: St Columbanus, St Aidan and St Kevin	156
Chapter 13: The Benefits of Walking With the Saints	169
Bibliography for Walking with the Saints	185

Introduction:

A Map for the Long Road Home

Fellow pilgrim,

Before we begin this third and final journey together, I feel I must be honest with you. The man who writes these words is not the man I always was. For many years, the only trinity I knew was violence, anger, and the cold, hard fist. My prayers were curses shouted into the uncaring night, and my communion was found in the bottom of a bottle or the fleeting, false warmth of a chemical haze. My life was a litany of blue lights, the sharp rap of a policeman's knuckles on a car window, and the sterile, echoing silence of a holding cell. I was a man at war with the world, but the truth is, the world was just a stand-in for the real enemy: myself.

I was a fighter, not in the noble sense of fighting for a cause, but in the brutal, animalistic sense of fighting for the sake of fighting. It was a language I understood. A clenched jaw, a tightened fist, the surge of adrenaline that momentarily drowned out the gnawing emptiness inside—this was my catechism. My body was a roadmap of my sins, a collection of scars from bar fights, street brawls, and the kind of stupid, pointless violence that blossoms in the dark soil of a broken spirit.

I was intimately familiar with the cold steel of handcuffs and the weary, disappointed sighs of police officers who knew me by name. My life was a revolving door of trouble, a self-fulfilling prophecy of rage and consequence. The drugs were just a way to numb the pain, to quiet the screaming void that my life had become. They were a cheap anaesthetic for a soul sickness that ran bone deep.

I tell you this not for dramatic effect, or to posture as some reformed tough guy. I tell you this because I need you to know that I have been in the desolate country. I have walked in the valley of the shadow of death and felt its cold breath on my neck. I know what it is to feel utterly and hopelessly lost, to believe that you are beyond the reach of grace, a ship so shattered it is fit only for the boneyard.

If you are reading these words and some part of you feels that same brokenness, that same sense of being a castaway on the shores of your own life, then know this: I am writing this for you. This entire book series is for you.

My transformation did not happen overnight. It was not a single, lightning-bolt moment of conversion, but a slow, quiet turning, like a great ship changing course in a vast ocean. It began not in a church, but in the woods. It began with the simple, profound discovery that became the heart of my first book, The Ever-Flowing Stream. In the depths of my despair, having burned every bridge and exhausted every escape route, I found myself walking in an old forest, the kind of place where the trees are ancient, and the silence is a living thing. For the first time in my life, I stopped. I stopped running, I stopped fighting, I stopped numbing myself. I just… stopped.

And in that stopping, I began to hear. I heard the rustle of leaves, the chatter of a squirrel, the gentle, persistent gurgle of a small stream making its way over moss-covered stones. There were no sermons, no choirs, no stained-glass windows. There was only the raw, unfiltered presence of God in His creation. This was the beginning of my healing. The Celtic Christians knew this truth intimately: that creation is the first cathedral, God's primary revelation of Himself. The ever-flowing stream became a metaphor for the grace I was so desperately thirsty for grace, which was always there, always flowing, waiting only for me to stoop down and drink.

Learning to see the world as sacred, as shimmering with the divine presence, began to change me from the inside out. The anger that had been my constant companion began to lose its grip. How can you remain consumed by rage when you are standing in a forest that feels like a sanctuary? How can you cling to violence when you are watching the delicate, determined dance of a spider weaving its web?

The practices I wrote about in The Ever-Flowing Stream—the daily walks, the quiet observation, the attunement to the seasons, the simple act of breathing in and out in a sacred place—were not just spiritual exercises; they were my lifeline. They were the slow, patient work of God rewiring my broken soul. The stream was washing me clean, not by erasing my past, but by showing me a new way to be present.

But a man cannot live by a stream alone, no matter how holy. The initial peace I found in nature was real, but it was solitary. My old life had been one of destructive, chaotic relationships, and my new life was becoming one of near-total isolation. I had traded the brawl of the pub for the silence of the woods, but I was still alone. I needed more than just a connection to creation; I needed a connection to people. I needed to learn how to be a man among men, not as a fighter, but as a brother. This is where the journey led me to the great, sturdy truth that became the heart of my second book, The Whisper of the Oak.

If the stream represented the ever-present flow of grace, the oak tree represented the rootedness, strength, and community I so desperately needed. It was in discovering the writings of the Celtic saints that I first encountered the concept of the anam cara, the "soul friend." This was a revelation. The idea of a friendship based not on posturing or shared vices, but on radical honesty, mutual accountability, and a shared journey toward God was utterly foreign to me. It was terrifying, and it was exactly what I needed.

Finding my own *anam cara* and learning to be one for others was the second great turning point in my life. It was in the safe space of this sacred friendship that I could finally be honest about the wreckage of my past. I could confess the violence, the anger, the shame, without fear of judgment. The oak tree became a symbol of the cruciform life—a life rooted in the earth of real, messy human community, with arms stretched wide in welcome, pointing always toward heaven.

Embracing the Cross was no longer an abstract theological concept; it was the daily act of dying to my old self—the fighter, the addict, the lone wolf—and rising to a new life of vulnerability, service, and love within a community. The practices in The Whisper of the Oak—the lectio divina, the fixed-hour prayers, the sharing of life in a small group—were the trellis that supported my fragile, growing faith. They gave structure to the grace I had discovered by the stream.

And so, here we are. We have journeyed from the stream to the oak. We have learned to find God in the solitude of nature and in the communion of soul friends. And yet, the journey is not over. The stream beckons us further, and the branches of that great oak reach toward a wider sky, inviting us to lift our eyes to the great cloud of witnesses who have walked this path before us, for I discovered on my own journey that even with a deep connection to creation and a loving community, there were still moments of profound loneliness. There were struggles and questions that my earthly friends, for all their love, could not fully understand. It was in these moments that I was led to the third and final truth of this trilogy: that the circle of *anam cara* extends beyond the visible horizon. In this book, we will learn that we are not only surrounded by a loving community on earth but also held, guided, and cherished by the entire communion of saints.

This is the story of Book Three. It is the story of how I, a broken man who once fought with his fists, learned to walk with saints. It is the story of how I discovered that St. Patrick, a man who knew the terror of being a captive in a foreign land, could understand my own feelings of being a prisoner to my past. It is the story of how St. Columba, a man of noble birth and fierce temper, could be a companion to me in my own struggle with anger. These were not distant, marble figures to me; they became my spiritual companions, my elder brothers, my soul friends in the vast, loving family of God.

But this is not a journey into abstract theology or distant history. This book is a practical guide, a map for the heart, showing how we can cultivate these sacred friendships in our own lives. We will learn to speak with the saints through the simple, honest language of prayer, transforming our spiritual practice from a solitary monologue into a rich and vibrant conversation. We will learn to listen for their wisdom and feel their presence through the quiet stillness of meditation, creating thin places in our own souls where heaven and earth can meet. And we will learn the ancient and powerful discipline of fasting, a practice that quiets the clamour of the world and the restlessness of our own minds, creating the sacred space necessary for these deep, transformative encounters. These are not complicated rituals for the spiritual elite; they are the accessible, time-honoured pathways of the heart, and we will walk them together, step by step.

And the fruits of this journey are profound. In a world that often feels isolating and chaotic, you will discover that you are never truly alone. You will find that the saints are not distant, marble figures, but living companions who offer their wisdom for your discernment, their courage for your struggles, and their prayers for your healing. This is not merely an intellectual exercise; it is a path to deep, personal transformation. By walking with the saints, you will find your own faith deepened, your sense of purpose clarified, and your heart expanded to embrace the vast, loving family of God that stretches across both heaven and earth. You will learn that the communion of saints is not a doctrine to be believed, but a living reality to be experienced, a wellspring of grace that nourishes and sustains the cruciform life.

My story is proof of this. The man who once worked as a bouncer and waited for fights now walks into a chapel looking for a friend—a friend like St. Kevin, who can teach me about stillness, or St. Brigid, who can teach me about hospitality. The hands that were once clenched in anger are now open in prayer. The path that once led to a Crown Court now leads to a monastery.

This is the transformation that is possible. This is the promise of the Gospel lived through the wisdom of the Celtic saints. It is a promise not only for me but also for you. No matter where you have been, no matter how broken you feel, there is a place for you in this great family. Soul friends are waiting to walk with you. The long road home is not meant to be walked alone. Come, let us walk it together.

The Three Books: A Trilogy of Transformation

Allow me to step back for a moment and show you how these three books fit together, how they form a complete map for the spiritual journey. Each book builds upon the last, and together they offer a comprehensive vision of Celtic Christian spirituality that is both ancient and urgently relevant to our modern world.

Book One: The Ever-Flowing Stream – Learning to Listen

The first book was about learning to listen. It was about recovering the lost art of paying attention to the sacred in the ordinary. In our modern world, we are drowning in noise—the constant buzz of notifications, the endless scroll of social media, the relentless demands of productivity and performance. We have become so addicted to distraction that we have forgotten how to be present simply. The Celtic Christians understood that before we can encounter God in Scripture or in community, we must first learn to encounter Him in creation. They called these sacred spaces "thin places"—locations where the veil between heaven and earth is gossamer-thin, where the presence of God is almost palpable.

In The Ever-Flowing Stream, I taught you how to find these thin places and how to create them in your own life. We learned to walk slowly, to observe the changing seasons, to see the fingerprints of God in the intricate design of a leaf or the patient persistence of a river carving its way through stone. We learned the practice of lectio naturae—reading the book of nature as we would read Scripture, allowing it to speak to us of the character and presence of God. We learned to pray with our bodies, to let the rhythm of our breath become a prayer, to let the act of walking become a pilgrimage.

This was the foundation. Without this capacity for stillness, for listening, for presence, all the other practices become hollow. You cannot pray deeply if you cannot be still. You cannot experience true community if you are constantly distracted. The stream taught us to slow down, to pay attention, to let the grace of God wash over us in the simple, ordinary moments of life. It taught us that God is not distant or abstract, but intimately present in the world He has made. This was the first transformation: from a life of noise and distraction to a life of attentiveness and presence.

Book Two: The Whisper of the Oak – Learning to Live

But presence alone is not enough. Once we have learned to listen, we must learn to live. This was the journey of the second book. If the stream represented the flow of grace, the oak tree represented the rootedness and strength required to live a truly Christian life in a broken world. The oak is a tree that grows slowly, sinking its roots deep into the earth, weathering storms, providing shelter and sustenance for countless creatures. It is a perfect image of the cruciform life—a life shaped by the Cross.

In The Whisper of the Oak, we explored what it means to live this cruciform life through the lens of Celtic Christian wisdom. We learned about the anam cara, the soul friend, and the profound importance of spiritual companionship. We learned that the Christian life is not meant to be lived in isolation, but in deep, honest, accountable relationships. We learned the daily practices that root us in our faith—the fixed-hour prayers that sanctify time, the lectio divina that allows Scripture to transform us, the rhythms of work and rest that honour the Sabbath. We learned to see our entire lives— our work, our relationships, our struggles, our joys—as the raw material of our sanctification. This was the second transformation: from a life of isolation and self-reliance to a life of community and interdependence. I learned that I could not heal alone, that I needed brothers and sisters to walk with me, to hold me accountable, to speak truth to me in love. The oak taught me that strength comes not from standing alone, but from being rooted in a community, from being part of something larger than myself. It taught me that the Cross is not just a symbol, but a way of life—a daily dying to self and rising to new life in Christ.

Book Three: The Communion of Saints – Learning to Belong

We now turn to the third book, the culmination of the journey. If the first book taught us to listen and the second taught us to live, this third book will teach us to belong. It will teach us that the community we discovered in Book Two extends far beyond the visible, earthly church. We are part of a vast, eternal family—the communion of saints—that includes not only our brothers and sisters on earth, but also the great cloud of witnesses who have gone before us.

This was the third great discovery of my own journey. As I grew in my faith and learned to pray and live in community, I began to feel a strange and wonderful sense of connection to the saints of old. I would read about St. Patrick's missionary journeys and feel as if he were speaking directly to me, encouraging me in my own work of sharing the Gospel. I would read about St. Columba's struggle with anger and pride, and I would feel less alone in my own struggles.

These were not just historical figures; they were companions, mentors, soul friends who had walked the same difficult path and who were now cheering me on from the other side.

But this connection did not happen automatically. It required intentionality. It required learning new practices—or rather, recovering ancient practices that the church had largely forgotten. This is what we will explore together in this book. We will learn how to cultivate these sacred friendships through the disciplines of prayer, meditation, and fasting. We will learn how to invoke the saints, not as a replacement for Christ, but as fellow pilgrims who point us always toward Him. We will learn how to listen for their wisdom, feel their presence, and draw strength from their example and intercession.

This is the third transformation: from a life of earthly belonging to a life of eternal belonging. We will learn that we are part of a family that transcends time and space, a family that includes the apostles and martyrs, the monks and mystics, the ordinary men and women who have faithfully followed Christ through the ages. We will learn that death is not the end of a relationship, but a transition. We will learn that the communion of saints is not a quaint doctrine but a living, breathing reality that can sustain, guide, and transform us.

Together, these three books form a complete vision of the Christian life. They teach us to listen, to live, and to belong. They teach us to find God in creation, in community, and in the communion of saints. They teach us that the spiritual life is not about escaping the world, but about learning to see the world as it truly is—sacred, shimmering with the presence of God, and teeming with companions, both seen and unseen, who are walking the same road toward the heart of God.

What This Book Will Do for You

Let me be very clear about what I am promising you in this book. This is not a work of abstract theology. This is not a historical survey of Celtic saints, though we will undoubtedly learn about them. This is not a book to be read and then placed on a shelf. This is a practical, hands-on guide to cultivating sacred friendships with the saints and, through those friendships, experiencing profound personal transformation.

You Will Learn to Pray in a New Way

Prayer is the foundation of spiritual life, but for many of us, prayer has become stale and lifeless. We recite the same words, make the same requests, and wonder why we feel so disconnected. In this book, you will learn to pray in a new way—or rather, in an ancient way that has been largely forgotten. You will learn to pray with the saints, not just to God. You will learn to invoke St. Patrick when you are facing a difficult mission, to call upon St. Brigid when you need to practice hospitality, and to seek the intercession of St. Columba when you are struggling with anger. You will learn that prayer is not a monologue, but a conversation. This rich, multi-layered conversation includes not only you and God, but also the entire communion of saints. This will transform your prayer life from a duty into a delight, from a solitary struggle into a communal celebration.
You Will Learn to Meditate and Encounter the Saints

Meditation is often misunderstood in Christian circles, dismissed as either too "Eastern" or too passive. But the Celtic Christians were masters of contemplative prayer, of the quiet, receptive stillness that allows us to hear the whisper of God. In this book, you will learn to meditate in the Celtic tradition—to create thin places in your own soul where heaven and earth can meet. You will learn to use icons and sacred images as windows into the eternal and as focal points for contemplation. You will learn to sit in silence and listen for the wisdom of the saints, to feel their presence, to receive their guidance. This is not about conjuring up visions or having mystical experiences (though God may grant those if He wills). This is about cultivating a receptive, attentive heart that is open to the movement of the Holy Spirit and the companionship of the saints.

You Will Learn the Transformative Power of Fasting

Fasting is among the most ancient and powerful spiritual disciplines, yet it is also among the most neglected in modern Christianity. We live in a culture of constant consumption, of endless indulgence, and we have forgotten the profound spiritual benefits of saying "no" to our appetites. In this book, you will learn to fast—not as a form of self-punishment or legalistic obligation, but as a way of creating sacred space in your life. Fasting quiets the noise of the world and the restlessness of your own mind. It heightens your spiritual sensitivity. It demonstrates your seriousness and commitment to God. When combined with prayer and meditation, fasting becomes a powerful way to deepen your connection with the saints and to experience transformative encounters with God.

You Will Discover You Are Not Alone

Perhaps the most important promise of this book is this: you will discover that you are not alone. In a world that is increasingly fragmented, isolated, and lonely, this message offers profound hope. You are part of a vast, eternal family. You have companions, mentors, and soul friends who understand your struggles because they have walked the same path. You have saints praying for you, encouraging you, and offering their wisdom and intercession. You are held, guided, and cherished by the entire communion of saints. This is not a metaphor or a nice sentiment. This is a living reality, and when you experience it, it will change everything.

You Will Be Transformed

Ultimately, this book is about transformation. It is about becoming the person God created you to be. For me, that transformation was dramatic—from a violent, drug-addicted criminal to a man of God who now teaches others. Your transformation may look different, but it will be no less real. By walking with the saints, by learning to pray, meditate, and fast, by opening yourself to the communion of saints, you will find your faith deepened, your character refined, your purpose clarified. You will find yourself becoming more patient, more loving, more courageous, more hopeful. You will find yourself becoming more like Christ, which is, after all, the goal of the Christian life.

This is not a quick fix or a magic formula. This is the work of a lifetime. But it is work that is deeply rewarding, work that will bear fruit in every area of your life. And you will not be doing this work alone. You will be walking with the saints, guided by their wisdom, sustained by their prayers, encouraged by their example. You will be part of the great, ongoing story of God's redemption, a story that began long before you were born and will continue long after you are gone. This is the promise of the communion of saints. This is the promise of this book.

An Invitation

Fellow pilgrim, I invite you to walk this road with me. I invite you to open your heart to the possibility that the communion of saints is not a distant doctrine, but a living reality. I invite you to learn the ancient practices of prayer, meditation, and fasting, and to discover for yourself the transformative power of walking with the saints. I invite you to join the great family of God, a family that stretches across time and space, a family that includes the broken and the healed, the sinners and the saints, the lost and the found.

This is the final book of the trilogy, but it is not the end of the journey. It is, in many ways, just the beginning. For once you have learned to listen (Book One), to live (Book Two), and to belong (Book Three), you will find that the road stretches out before you, endless and inviting. You will find that there is always more grace to receive, more love to give, more transformation to experience. The ever-flowing stream never runs dry. The oak tree continues to grow. And the communion of saints is always there, waiting to welcome you home.

Come, let us walk together. The saints are waiting.

Stuart McGhie

How to Use This Book

Before we begin, let me offer some practical guidance on how to approach this book. This is not a book to be rushed through. It is not a book to be read in a weekend and then set aside. This is a book to be lived with, returned to again and again, worked through slowly and intentionally.

Read with an Open Heart

First, I ask that you read with an open mind. Some of what I share in this book may challenge your preconceptions about the saints, about prayer, about the nature of the Christian life. You may come from a tradition that has been suspicious of the saints, viewing any devotion to them as dangerously close to idolatry. I understand that hesitation. I felt it myself. But I ask you to set aside your assumptions, at least temporarily, and to approach this material with curiosity and openness. The communion of saints is a biblical doctrine, rooted in the New Testament and practised by Christians for two thousand years. It is not a Catholic innovation or a Celtic peculiarity. It is part of our shared heritage as followers of Christ.

Practice as You Read

Second, I encourage you to practice as you read. Each chapter of this book includes not only teaching, but also practical exercises and spiritual disciplines. Do not skip these. Do not tell yourself you will come back to them later. The transformation I am promising you will not come from reading about these practices; it will come from doing them. Set aside time each day to pray with the saints, to meditate, to fast. Start small if you need to. Even five or ten minutes of intentional practice per day can begin to change you. As you grow more comfortable with these disciplines, you can expand them, deepen them, and make them your own.

Find a Companion

Third, if at all possible, find a companion to walk this road with you. The Celtic Christians understood that the spiritual life is not meant to be lived in isolation. Find an anam cara, a soul friend, who can read this book with you, practice these disciplines with you, and hold you accountable. Meet regularly to discuss what you are learning, share your struggles and breakthroughs, and pray together. If you cannot find someone in person, consider joining an online community or finding a spiritual director who can guide you. The journey is always richer when it is shared.

Be Patient with Yourself

Fourth, be patient with yourself. Transformation takes time. You will not master these practices overnight. You will have days when prayer feels dry, when meditation feels impossible, when fasting feels like a burden. This is normal. This is part of the process. Do not be discouraged. The saints themselves struggled with these same challenges. St. Columba struggled with his temper throughout his life. St. Patrick faced doubt and loneliness. St. Kevin struggled to balance his love of solitude with his call to community. You are in good company. Keep showing up. Keep practicing. Keep opening your heart to the grace of God and the companionship of the saints. Over time, you will begin to see the fruit.

Return to the Stream and the Oak

Finally, I encourage you to return to the first two books in this trilogy as needed. The practices in this book build upon the foundations laid in The Ever-Flowing Stream and The Whisper of the Oak. If you find yourself struggling to remain still during meditation, return to Book One and revisit the practices of attentiveness and presence. If you find yourself feeling isolated on your spiritual journey, return to Book Two to reconnect with the importance of community and the anam cara. These three books are intended to work together, reinforcing and deepening one another. They constitute a comprehensive map of the spiritual journey, and you may find yourself returning to different parts of it at different stages of your life.

A Final Word

I began this preface by telling you about the man I used to be—a man of violence, anger, and addiction. I want to end by telling you about the man I am becoming. I am still a work in progress. I still struggle. I still fail. But I am not the man I was. The transformation is real and ongoing.

I am a man who has learned to find God in the silence of a forest and in the laughter of a friend.

I am a man who has learned to pray not just with words, but with my whole life. I am a man who has learned that I am part of a family that stretches across heaven and earth, a family that includes St. Patrick and St. Brigid, St. Columba and St. Kevin, and countless others whose names I do not yet know but whose presence I feel.

I am a man who has been saved by grace, sustained by community, and transformed by the communion of saints. And I am a man who now spends his life teaching others this same path, sharing this same hope, offering this same invitation.

This is my story. But it is not just my story. It is the story of every person who has ever felt lost and been found, who has ever felt broken and been healed, who has ever felt alone and discovered they were surrounded by love. It is the story of the Gospel, lived out in the particular, beautiful, challenging tradition of Celtic Christianity.

And now, it is your story too.

Welcome to the family.

Welcome to the communion of saints.

Welcome home.

Let us begin.

Chapter 1:

The Communion of Saints: From Doctrine to Lived Reality

I remember the moment the floor fell out from under me. It wasn't in a bar fight, or in the back of a police car, or in the hazy aftermath of a drug-fueled night. It was years after all that. Years after I had first stumbled out of the darkness and into the quiet, cleansing presence of God, I found by The Ever-Flowing Stream.

Years after I had begun to build a new life, rooted in the community of The Whisper of the Oak. By all outward appearances, I was a new man. I was leading a small Bible study, teaching others about the very grace that had saved me. And I felt like a complete and utter fraud.

We were sitting in a circle in the small, cluttered basement of our church, the air thick with the smell of stale coffee and earnest faith. A young man, his face a roadmap of the same kind of pain I knew so well, was sharing his story. It was a story of addiction, of broken relationships, of a deep, gnawing emptiness that the world could not fill. He was looking at me, his eyes pleading for an answer, for some hope that his life could be different. And in that moment, I was paralysed. Who was I to offer this man hope? I was a charlatan, a wolf in sheep's clothing.

The ghosts of my past rose up to mock me—the flash of blue lights, the sting of pepper spray, the cold, brutal finality of a cell door slamming shut. The man I used to be was standing right behind the man I was pretending to be, whispering in my ear: You have no right to be here. You are a fake. You are still the same violent, broken man you always were.

I mumbled some platitudes, some half-hearted words of encouragement that sounded hollow even to my own ears. The meeting ended, and I fled into the night, my heart pounding with a familiar cocktail of shame and fear. I drove to the woods, the same woods that had been my first sanctuary, the place where I had first learned to listen for God. But that night, the woods were silent. The stream offered no comfort. The oak tree gave no strength. I was utterly alone, adrift on a sea of my own inadequacy.

I went home, defeated. I couldn't pray. The words wouldn't come. I felt like a failure, not just as a teacher, but as a Christian. I had come so far, and yet I felt as if I had gone nowhere at all. In desperation, I picked up a book I had been given, a collection of stories about the Celtic saints. I had thumbed through it before but had found the stories quaint and irrelevant, the stuff of myth and legend. But that night, I had nowhere else to turn.

I opened the book at random and began to read about St. Patrick. I knew the cartoon version, of course—the man who drove the snakes out of Ireland. But this was different. This was the story of a man who had been kidnapped as a teenager, sold into slavery, and forced to work as a shepherd in a cold, hostile land. A man who had felt the terror of captivity, the gnawing loneliness of exile. A man who, after escaping and returning home, felt an irresistible call from God to go back to the very people who had enslaved him, to bring them the Gospel of love and forgiveness.

As I read, something began to shift inside me. I read Patrick's own words from his Confession:

"I was like a stone lying in the deep mud; and He that is mighty came, and in His mercy lifted me up."

A stone in the deep mud. That was it. That was me. I wasn't a fraud pretending to be a saint; I was a stone that had been lifted out of the mud. Patrick wasn't a plaster saint on a dashboard; he was a man who knew the deep mud. He knew what it was to be a captive. I had been a captive too—a captive to my anger, my addiction, my past. And yet, God had used him. God had taken this broken, traumatised man and used him to transform a nation.

In that moment, sitting alone in my small, quiet house, I felt a strange and wonderful sense of companionship. I was not alone in my struggle. I was not the first broken man God had called to serve Him. Patrick knew. He understood. It was not an audible voice, nor a vision, nor a mystical experience. It was something quieter, deeper. It was a sense of solidarity, of kinship. It was the feeling of a hand on my shoulder, a whisper in my soul: You are not alone. I have been here too. Keep going.

I didn't have a name for what I was feeling that night. I only knew it was real and had saved me from the brink of despair. But the Church has had a name for it for two thousand years. It is called the communion of saints.

What We Mean by "Communion of Saints"

For many of us, particularly those from a Protestant background, the phrase "communion of saints" is something we recite in the Apostles' Creed without much thought. It is a doctrine, a theological concept, a line in a dusty old confession. It is not a living, breathing reality. We think of the saints, if we think of them at all, as historical figures, as stained-glass portraits, as characters in a book. They are the spiritual all-stars, the heroes of the faith, admirable but distant, long dead and gone. We may honour their memory, but the idea of having a relationship with them, of them being active and present in our lives, feels strange, foreign, perhaps even a little bit dangerous.

But this is not what the Church has believed for two millennia. The communion of saints is not a dusty doctrine; it is a family reunion. It is the profound and beautiful truth that the Church is one body, united in Christ, and that this body is not divided by death. The author of the letter to the Hebrews paints a breathtaking picture of this reality.

After listing the great heroes of the faith in chapter 11—Abel, Enoch, Noah, Abraham, Sarah, Moses, and so on—he concludes in chapter 12:

"Therefore, since we are surrounded by so great a cloud of witnesses, let us also lay aside every weight, and sin which clings so closely, and let us run with endurance the race that is set before us, looking to Jesus, the founder and perfecter of our faith." (Hebrews 12:1-2a)

Think about that image. We are running a race, a difficult, gruelling marathon. And in the stands, surrounding the track, is a great cloud of witnesses. They are not passive spectators. They are cheering us on. They are leaning over the rails, shouting our names, encouraging us, urging us to keep going. They know the race's difficulty because they have run it themselves. They have faced the same struggles, temptations, and moments of despair. And they are here with us, in this very moment, as we run our own race.

This is the communion of saints. It is the family of God, stretching across time and space, united in the mystical body of Christ. The Apostle Paul speaks of this in his letter to the Ephesians: "So then you are no longer strangers and aliens, but you are fellow citizens with the saints and members of the household of God" (Ephesians 2:19). We are not just followers of a religion; we are members of a household, citizens of a kingdom. And that household includes not only the people we see in the pews on Sunday morning, but also the apostles and martyrs, the monks and mystics, the ordinary men and women who have faithfully followed Christ through the ages.

Death, in this understanding, is not a wall that separates us, but a veil that thins. Those who have gone before us are not gone; they are simply in another room of the same house. They are more alive than we are, living in the full, unmediated presence of God. And because they are in Christ, and we are in Christ, we are still connected. We are still one family. The love that binds us together in the body of Christ is stronger than death.

This is a truth that the Celtic Christians understood in their bones. For them, the veil between heaven and earth was always thin. The saints were not distant figures; they were family. They were the elder siblings and spiritual mentors, the companions on the journey. They were present in the landscape, in the turning of the seasons, in the daily rhythms of work and prayer. To walk with the saints was not a strange or esoteric practice; it was as natural as breathing.

Why This Matters for Your Life

This may all sound beautiful, you may be thinking, but what does it have to do with my life? What does it have to do with my struggles, my loneliness, my quiet desperation? It has everything to do with it.

We are living in the midst of a profound epidemic of loneliness. Despite being more connected than ever through technology, we are more isolated than ever. We have thousands of "friends" on social media, but we have forgotten how to be friends in real life. We live in a culture of radical individualism, one that tells us we must be self-sufficient, pull ourselves up by our own bootstraps, and be the masters of our own destiny. And it is killing us. It is leaving us anxious, depressed, and utterly alone.

I know this loneliness intimately. As I noted in the preface, chaotic, destructive relationships marked my previous life. When I came to faith, I swung to the other extreme. I found peace in the solitude of nature, but I was still alone. In The Whisper of the Oak, I wrote about the life-changing discovery of the anam cara, the soul friend, and the importance of living in community. And that was, and is, essential. We need flesh-and-blood people to walk with us, to hold us accountable, to love us in our messiness.

But even with a deep connection to creation and a loving community, there were still moments when I felt profoundly alone. There were struggles in my heart that I could not fully articulate to my earthly friends. There were battles with my old demons—the anger, the shame, the memory of violence—that felt unique to me. In those moments, my few friends could offer comfort, but they could not fully understand. They had not walked in my shoes. They had not been in the deep mud.

This is where the communion of saints became not just a beautiful idea, but a lifeline. When I was wrestling with my fierce temper, a temper that had once landed me in jail, I began to read about St. Columba. Here was a man of God, a founder of monasteries, a great missionary—and he had a legendary temper. He was a man of noble birth, proud and passionate, and his anger once sparked a battle that claimed thousands of lives. As a penance, he was exiled from his beloved Ireland, and he spent the rest of his life on the small island of Iona, struggling to tame the beast within him. He never fully succeeded. Even in his old age, his fellow monks knew to tread carefully around him. But he never stopped fighting. He never gave up. He clung to Christ and allowed God to use him, including his anger.

Reading about Columba, I felt a profound sense of relief. I was not a monster. I was not alone. Here was a saint, a hero of the faith, who understood my struggle from within. I began to talk to him, to ask for his prayers. "Columba," I would say, "you know what this is like. Pray for me. Help me." And in those moments, I felt his companionship. I felt his solidarity. I felt his encouragement to keep fighting, to keep clinging to Christ, to believe that God could use even a broken, angry man like me.

This is what the communion of saints offers us. It offers us mentors who have walked the path before us. It offers us companions who understand our specific struggles. It provides intercessors who pray for us in the very presence of God. It offers us proof that transformation is possible, that even the most broken people can become saints.

In a world that tells you that you are alone, the communion of saints declares that you are part of a vast, loving family. In a world that tells you that you must be perfect, the saints show you that God uses broken, struggling people. In a world that tells you that your past defines you, the saints demonstrate that grace can rewrite your story. This is not just a nice idea. This is the good news that can save your life. It saved mine.

Common Misconceptions

Before we proceed, we must address common misconceptions and fears surrounding this topic, particularly among those of us from a Protestant background. These were my own fears, and it is important to face them head-on.

"Isn't this idolatry? Aren't we supposed to worship God alone?"

Yes, absolutely. We are to worship God alone. The communion of saints is not about worshipping the saints. The Church has always made a clear distinction between latria (the worship due to God alone) and dulia (the veneration or honour given to the saints). We do not worship the saints. We honour them as heroes of the faith, as our elder brothers and sisters, as members of our own family. We ask for their prayers in the same way we would ask a living friend to pray for us. When I ask my friend John to pray for me, I am not worshipping John. I am acknowledging that we are part of the same body, and that we are called to bear one another's burdens. Asking St. Columba to pray for me is no different. In fact, he is in a much better position to pray for me, as he is living in the full, unfiltered presence of God.

"Isn't this a Catholic practice? I'm not Catholic."

While the Catholic and Orthodox churches have maintained a more visible and robust practice of the communion of saints, it is not theirs alone. It is part of our shared Christian heritage. The doctrine is rooted in Scripture and was practised by the early church long before the divisions of the Reformation. The Celtic Christians, who were active long before the major splits in the church, had a vibrant and beautiful practice of walking with the saints. As Protestants, we rightly emphasise the importance of Scripture and a personal relationship with Jesus Christ. But in our zeal to correct the excesses of the medieval church, we have sometimes thrown the baby out with the bathwater. We have cut ourselves off from the wisdom, the companionship, and the prayers of the great cloud of witnesses. It is time to recover this lost treasure of our faith.

"Doesn't this diminish Christ's unique role as mediator?"

The New Testament is clear: "For there is one God, and there is one mediator between God and men, the man Christ Jesus" (1 Timothy 2:5). Christ is the one and only mediator of our salvation. He is the bridge between God and humanity. Nothing and no one can replace Him. But asking a saint to pray for us does not replace Christ as mediator; it affirms our participation in His body. When we pray for one another, we are participating in Christ's own mediatorial work. The saints, as members of His body who are now perfected in heaven, participate in this work more profoundly.

They do not pray in their own name or by their own power. They pray in the name of Jesus and by the power of His Spirit. Their prayers, like ours, are effective only because of Christ's work on the Cross. The saints do not draw us away from Christ; they draw us closer to Him. They are like the moon, which has no light of its own but reflects the sun's. The saints reflect the light of Christ, and in seeing them, we see Him more clearly.

A Living Reality, Not a Distant Doctrine

My hope in this book is to guide you from an intellectual understanding of the communion of saints to a lived experience of it. I want you to know in your bones that you are not alone. I want you to experience the companionship of the saints in your own life, in your own struggles, in your own journey of transformation.

This is not about learning a new set of religious rules or rituals. This is about opening your heart to a relationship. It is about learning to see with new eyes, to listen with new ears. It is about discovering that the family of God is larger, more vibrant, and more present than you ever imagined.

My own story is proof that this is possible. The man who once walked into a bar looking for a fight now walks into a chapel looking for a friend—a friend like St. Patrick, who can teach me about courage, or St. Brigid, who can teach me about hospitality, or St. Columba, who can sit with me in my struggle with anger. The hands that were once clenched in violence are now open in prayer. The path that once led to a jail cell now leads to a monastery. This is the transformation that is possible when we open ourselves to the grace of God, which flows to us not only directly but also through the hands and hearts of our brothers and sisters, both in heaven and on earth.

This is not a journey for the spiritual elite. This is a journey for ordinary, broken people like you and me. It is a journey for those who are tired of being alone, for those who are hungry for something more, for those who dare to believe that the promises of God are true. The communion of saints is not a doctrine to be believed, but a living reality to be experienced, a wellspring of grace that nourishes and sustains the cruciform life.

So, I invite you to take the first step. You don't need to have it all figured out. You don't need to have all your theological questions answered. You need a little bit of curiosity, a little bit of courage, and a willingness to try.

Practices for This Chapter

1. A Simple Prayer: Throughout this week, I invite you to begin a simple practice. Each morning, before you start your day, find a quiet place and pray these words: "Great cloud of witnesses, surround me today. Pray for me as I run my race." That's it. You don't need to feel anything. You don't need to have a mystical experience. Just offer the prayer. Open the door, just a crack, to the possibility that you are not alone.

2. Find a Companion: Think about your own life, your own struggles, your own hopes. Is there a particular challenge you are facing right now? A particular virtue you are trying to cultivate? A particular mission you feel called to? Go to the appendix of this book, or do a simple search online, and find a saint who struggled with the same thing. Read a short biography of that saint. Learn their story.

And then, begin to pray this simple prayer: "St. [Name], you know what this is like. Pray for me." See what happens. Just see.

This is where the journey begins, not with a grand theological treatise, but with a simple, honest prayer. It is the first step on the long road home, a road that we do not have to walk alone. The saints are waiting. Let us begin.

The Celtic Worldview: A World Alive with Presence

To truly grasp why the communion of saints was so central to Celtic Christians, we must step back and see the world as they did. This is a journey back to the very heart of The Ever-Flowing Stream, to the foundational truth that creation is not a neutral, lifeless backdrop for human drama, but a living, breathing sacrament, shimmering with the presence of God.

In our modern, post-Enlightenment world, we have been trained to see the world as a machine. We have divided reality into neat, separate categories: the natural and the supernatural, the physical and the spiritual, the sacred and the secular. We have disenchanted the world, stripping it of its mystery and its magic. God, if He exists at all, is a distant, clockmaker God who set the universe in motion and then stepped back to watch it run. He is "up there," and we are "down here." The spiritual world is a separate, invisible realm that only occasionally, and miraculously, intersects with our own.

This worldview would have been utterly foreign to the Celtic Christians. For them, there was no sharp division between the spiritual and the physical. The world was alive, charged with the grandeur of God. Heaven and earth were not two separate realities, but two dimensions of the same reality, and the veil between them was thin. This is the concept of the "thin place" that we explored in Book One—a place where the spiritual world seems to break through into the physical, where the presence of God is almost palpable. But for the Celtic Christians, it was not just certain places that were thin; the whole world was thin.

The whole world was a sacrament.

This is why they were so attuned to nature. They saw the face of Christ in the rising sun, they heard the voice of the Spirit in the wild goose, they felt the embrace of the Father in the strength of the oak. Creation was not a resource to be exploited; it was a revelation to be received. It was the first Bible, the primary scripture, written in the language of mountains and rivers, of stars and seasons.

When you live in a world that is this alive, this permeable to the spiritual, the communion of saints is not a difficult doctrine to accept. It is a natural, logical extension of your experience. If God is present in the stream and the tree, why would He not be present in His people? If the veil between heaven and earth is thin, why would it be a thick, impenetrable wall for those who have passed from this life into the next? If the body of Christ is one, why would death have the power to sever its bonds?

For the Celtic Christians, the saints were simply the part of the family that had moved into the next room. They were still present, still part of the community, still engaged in the life of the church. They were the elder brothers and sisters who had finished the race and were now cheering from the stands. They were the spiritual mentors who could be called upon for wisdom and guidance. They were the powerful intercessors who had the King's ear. To ignore them, to act as if they were not there, would have been as strange as ignoring the living, breathing presence of the forest or the sea.

This is a radical, countercultural way of seeing the world. It challenges our modern assumptions about reality. It invites us to re-enchant our world, to see it not as a collection of dead objects, but as a living sacrament, teeming with the presence of God and His saints. It invites us to believe that we are not alone, that we are part of a vast, interconnected family, a great dance of creation and redemption that includes the stars and the stones, the angels and the archangels, the living and the dead.

My own journey into this worldview was slow and halting. The man who once saw the world as a hostile, dog-eat-dog jungle had to learn to see it as a sanctuary. The man who once saw other people as either threats or opportunities had to learn to see them as brothers and sisters. And the man who once saw death as the final, terrifying end had to learn to see it as a thin veil, a doorway into a larger life.

It was the quiet, patient work of God, begun in the solitude of the woods and continued in the community of the church. And it was the companionship of the saints that helped me to believe it was all true. When I read about St. Kevin, who was so still in prayer that a blackbird nested in his outstretched hand, I began to believe that nature really could be a friend. When I read about St. Brigid, who could hang her cloak on a sunbeam, I began to believe that the physical world was not as solid and predictable as I had thought. And when I read about St. Patrick, who felt Christ's presence in every breath, I began to believe that I, too, could live in constant communion with God.

The saints were my guides into this new, enchanted world. They were the proof that it was real. They had lived it. And in walking with them, I began to live it too. This is the invitation of Celtic Christianity. This is the invitation of this book. It is an invitation to come home—home to a world that is alive with the presence of God, home to a family that stretches across heaven and earth, home to the deep, abiding truth that you are never, ever alone.

A Deeper Look at My Own Journey

Let me take you back to that night, the night the floor fell out from under me. Let me tell you more about the man who sat in that church basement, feeling like a fraud. To understand the power of the communion of saints, you must understand the depth of the loneliness it heals.

I had built a new life. I had a wife, a home, and a job. I was, by all accounts, a success story, a testament to God's grace. But inside, I was still the same scared, angry kid from the streets. I had learned to put on a good face, to say the right things, to play the part of the reformed man. But it was a performance. I was terrified that at any moment, someone would see through the mask, that they would see the violence that still simmered beneath the surface, the shame that still clung to me like a shroud.

The young man in the Bible study—his name was Mark—was a mirror. When I looked at him, I saw myself. I saw the same haunted eyes, the same desperate hunger for something real. And when he looked at me, he was looking for a father, a mentor, a guide. He was looking for someone who had made it to the other side. And I knew, with a sickening certainty, that I was still drowning.

My mumbled platitudes were not just a failure of nerve; they were a betrayal. I was offering him a cheap, second-hand map to a country I had not yet fully explored myself. I was pointing to a destination I was not sure I could ever reach. The shame of that moment was a physical thing. It burned in my chest, it tightened my throat, it made my hands tremble. I fled the church that night not just because I was a fraud, but because I was a coward.

Reading about St. Patrick that night was like a drowning man finding a life raft. It wasn't just the parallels between his story and mine—the captivity, the loneliness, the sense of being an outsider. It was his honesty. In his Confession, Patrick is not a plaster saint. He is a real, flesh-and-blood man, full of self-doubt and insecurity. He calls himself "unlearned" and "a sinner, the most rustic and the least of all the faithful." He worries that he is not eloquent enough, not holy enough, not worthy of the excellent task God has given him. He is, in other words, a man who felt like a fraud.

And yet, he went. He answered the call. He returned to the land of his captors, a land he had every reason to hate, and he loved them. He loved them with a fierce, stubborn, reckless love that could only have come from God. He did not do it because he was confident in his own abilities. He did it because he was confident in God. "I am not worthy," he seems to say on every page, "but He is."

This was the message my soul needed to hear. My problem was not that I was a fraud; my problem was that I was still trying to be the hero of my own story. I was still relying on my own strength, my own wisdom, my own righteousness. I was trying to be the man Mark needed me to be, instead of pointing him to the Man who could save us both. Patrick taught me that night that the power of our witness does not lie in our perfection, but in our brokenness. It lies in our willingness to admit that we are stones in the deep mud, and to point to the mighty One who has lifted us up.

My conversation with Patrick did not end that night. It was just the beginning. He has become my constant companion in ministry. When I feel inadequate, I remember his humility. When I feel afraid, I remember his courage. When I am tempted to give up, I remember his persistence. He is not a distant historical figure to me. He is my anam cara, my soul friend, my elder brother who walks with me, prays for me, and shows me the way.

This is what it means to move from doctrine to lived reality. It is the difference between reading a biography of a great leader and having that leader as your personal mentor. It is the difference between studying a map and walking the road. The communion of saints is not a theory to be debated; it is a relationship to be cultivated.

And it is a relationship that has the power to heal our deepest wounds, to calm our greatest fears, and to transform our lives from the inside out.

This is the journey I am inviting you on in this book. It is a journey that saved my life, and I believe it can save yours too. It is a journey into the heart of the family of God, a journey into the deep, abiding truth that you are loved, you are cherished, and you are never, ever alone.

Chapter 2:

The Saints: Who They Are and Why They Matter

For a long time, the saints were a problem for me. Even after my encounter with St. Patrick, which had been a genuine lifeline in a moment of crisis, I kept them at arm's length. My Protestant upbringing had installed a kind of silent alarm in my soul that went off whenever I got too close to anything that felt "Catholic." The saints, with their statues and their feast days and their litanies, felt decidedly on the wrong side of that line. They felt like a distraction from what really mattered: Jesus. My relationship with God was direct, personal, and unmediated. I didn't need a committee of dead people to get in the way.

But there was another, deeper reason for my resistance. The saints, as I understood them, were perfect. They were spiritual superheroes, men and women of flawless virtue and unshakable faith. They were the marble statues in old cathedrals, their faces serene and otherworldly, their hands perpetually folded in prayer. They were, in short, everything I was not. What could I, a man whose past was a litany of violence and addiction, a man who still wrestled daily with a ferocious temper, possibly have in common with these paragons of holiness? Their perfection did not inspire me; it intimidated me. It highlighted my own brokenness and inadequacy. They were not companions for the journey; they were the impossible standard I could never hope to reach.

I might have stayed in that place of respectful distance, admiring the saints from afar but never daring to get close, if it hadn't been for St. Columba. And my encounter with him was not one of gentle invitation, but of brutal, head-on collision.

I was in a rage. It was a familiar feeling, a hot, white fire that started in my gut and consumed everything in its path. The trigger was something trivial—a perceived slight, a careless word, I don't even remember what. But it tapped into a deep well of anger that was always just beneath the surface, a remnant of the man I used to be. My fists were clenched, my jaw was tight, and I was pacing my small study like a caged animal. I wanted to break something. I wanted to hurt someone. The old, violent instincts were roaring back to life, and I was terrified.

In that moment, I was a million miles away from the gentle, contemplative man I was trying to be. The peace I had found by the stream, the community I had built under the oak—it all felt like a lie. I was a monster, a fraud, a man pretending to be good while a beast raged within.

I collapsed into my chair, exhausted and ashamed. My eyes fell on the same book of Celtic saints that had introduced me to Patrick. I picked it up, not with any hope, but with a kind of self-loathing curiosity. I wanted to see just how far I was from these perfect people. I flipped through the pages, my anger still simmering, and my eyes landed on a name: Columba.

I began to read, and the story that unfolded was not what I expected. Columba was a prince, a poet, a scholar, a man of immense charisma and spiritual power. He founded monasteries, he advised kings, and he performed miracles. He was, by any measure, a spiritual giant. But he was also a man of fierce pride and a volcanic temper. The story goes that he became embroiled in a dispute with another monk over the right to copy a psalter. The dispute escalated; a king intervened, and Columba, in his pride and fury, incited a battle. It was a bloody, brutal affair, and thousands of men were killed. All because of a book. All because of one man's pride.

As a penance for his sin, Columba was exiled from his beloved Ireland. He was sent to the small, windswept island of Iona, off the coast of Scotland, with a mission to convert as many souls to Christ as had died in the battle he caused. He spent the rest of his life on that rocky outcrop, building a community that would become a beacon of light for all of Europe. But he never fully conquered his temper. His fellow monks knew him as a man of deep love and profound wisdom, but they also knew to give him a wide berth when his Irish fire was up.

I sat there, stunned. The rage that had been consuming me just moments before began to recede, replaced by a wave of stunned recognition. Columba, the great saint, the founder of Iona, the Dove of the Church—he was like me. He knew this fire. He knew this pride. He knew the shame of seeing your own sin cause devastation. He wasn't a marble statue. He was a man of flesh and blood, a man who wrestled with the same demons that I did. And God had not abandoned him. God had not disqualified him. God had taken his broken, passionate, angry heart and used it for His glory.

In that moment, Columba became more real to me than any living person. He was not a historical figure; he was a brother. He was a fellow struggler. He was an anam cara who reached across fifteen centuries to sit with me in my shame and tell me, "I know. I have been here too. Do not give up."

That was the day the saints stopped being a problem for me and started being a lifeline. That was the day I realised that the communion of saints is not a club for the perfect, but a hospital for the broken. It is a hospital where the doctors are former patients, the ones who know the disease from the inside out. They are not intimidating paragons of virtue; they are our elder brothers and sisters, scarred and beautiful, who have finished the race and are now turning back to cheer us on.

Who Are the Saints?

My encounter with St. Columba shattered my preconceived notions of what it means to be a saint. I had always thought of saints as a special, elite class of Christians, a spiritual hall of fame reserved for the best and the brightest. But the word "saint" (in Greek, hagios) means "holy one" or "set apart one." In the New Testament, it is a word used to describe all believers, not just a select few. Paul begins his letter to the Ephesians, "To the saints who are in Ephesus, and are faithful in Christ Jesus." He writes to the Philippians, "To all the saints in Christ Jesus who are at Philippi." For Paul, if you are in Christ, you are a saint. You are a holy one, set apart by God for His purposes.

So, in the broadest sense, the communion of saints includes every person who has ever placed their faith in Jesus Christ. It is the great, sprawling, messy, beautiful family of God, from the apostles to the martyrs, from the desert fathers to the medieval mystics, from the great reformers to the quiet, faithful grandmother who taught you how to pray. It is the "great cloud of witnesses" that surrounds us, a crowd so vast that the author of Revelation describes it as "a great multitude that no one could number, from every nation, from all tribes and peoples and languages, standing before the throne and before the Lamb" (Revelation 7:9).

This is our family. This is our heritage. We are not the first to walk this path. We are part of a long, unbroken chain of faith, a river of grace that has been flowing through history for two thousand years. To be a Christian is to be a member of this family, to be a citizen of this kingdom, to be a part of this great cloud of witnesses.

Within this vast family, however, there are some whose lives have shone with a particular brightness, whose stories have been preserved and passed down through the generations as a source of inspiration and encouragement. These are the men and women we typically think of as "the saints"—the ones who have been formally recognised by the church for their heroic virtue and their powerful witness to the Gospel. They are not a different category of Christian; they are simply the elder brothers and sisters whose lives have become signposts for the rest of us, pointing us toward Christ.

In this book, we focus primarily on a particular branch of this family tree: the Celtic saints. These are the men and women who lived in Ireland, Scotland, Wales, and England during the early Middle Ages, a time of great cultural upheaval and spiritual vitality. They are saints like Patrick and Brigid, Columba and Aidan, Kevin and Hilda. And as we will see, they are a group of saints who are particularly well-suited to be our companions in the modern world.

The Celtic Saints: A Brief Introduction

Why focus on the Celtic saints? What makes them so special? As we explored in the previous chapter, the Celtic Christians had a unique and beautiful worldview. They lived in a world alive with the presence of God, a world in which the veil between heaven and earth was thin. This gave their spirituality a particular flavour, an earthy, poetic, passionate quality that is deeply attractive to many of us today.

Their saints reflect this worldview. The Celtic saints are not, for the most part, ethereal, otherworldly figures. They are men and women of the earth. They are poets and farmers, scholars and sailors, abbots and abbesses who are deeply engaged with the world around them. They are passionate, strong-willed, and intensely human. They get angry, they get discouraged, they make mistakes. They are, in other words, a lot like us.

This is what makes them so accessible. When we read their stories, we do not feel the intimidating distance of perfection. We feel the comforting shock of recognition. We see our own struggles, passions, and brokenness reflected in their lives. And in seeing how God worked through them, in all their messy humanity, we begin to believe that He can work through us too.

Throughout this book, we will learn about many of these Celtic companions. But for now, let me briefly introduce you to the six who will be our primary guides:

• **St. Patrick:** The Apostle of Ireland, a man who was kidnapped into slavery and returned to love and forgive his captors. He is a companion for those called to a difficult mission, for those who need courage, and for those learning to forgive.

• **St. Brigid:** The "Mary of the Gael," a woman of immense generosity, hospitality, and spiritual power. She is a companion for those learning to open their hearts and homes, for those seeking to integrate their faith with their creativity, and for those called to care for the poor and the marginalised.

• **St. Columba:** The Dove of the Church, a prince and a poet, a man of immense spiritual gifts who wrestled with a fierce temper his entire life. He is a companion for all of us who struggle with anger, pride, and the consequences of our own sin.

• **St. Columbanus:** The fiery missionary who left Ireland to re-evangelise a Europe that had fallen into darkness. He is a companion for those called to be prophetic witnesses, for those who need the courage to speak truth to power, and for those navigating times of change and upheaval.

• **St. Aidan:** The gentle apostle of Northumbria, a man known for his humility, his simplicity, and his deep love for the poor. He is a companion for those who are learning to share their faith with gentleness and respect, and for those who are seeking to live a simpler, more incarnational life.

• **St. Kevin:** The hermit of Glendalough, a man who fled to the wilderness to live in deep communion with God and creation. He is a companion for those seeking to cultivate a deeper contemplative life, for those learning to find God in silence and solitude, and for those who feel a deep connection to the natural world.

These are just a few of the many friends who are waiting to meet you. They are not a pantheon of gods to be appeased, but a circle of friends to be embraced. They are the elder brothers and sisters who have walked this path before us, and they are eager to share their wisdom, their prayers, and their companionship with us as we walk it now.

Why the Saints Matter

So, why does this matter? Why should we bother getting to know these long-dead figures from a distant time and place? The saints matter for at least four reasons:

1. They are Models and Archetypes.

The saints show us what a life lived for Christ looks like in the flesh. They are not abstract ideals, but concrete examples. They show us how to be courageous in the face of fear (Patrick), generous in a world of scarcity (Brigid), and honest about our struggles (Columba). They embody the virtues we are trying to cultivate. They are archetypes of the Christian life, living icons of what it means to be fully human and fully alive in Christ.

When we don't know how to live, we can look to them and learn.

2. They are Companions Who Understand Our Struggles.

This, for me, is the most powerful reason of all. The saints are not perfect. They were broken, struggling human beings, just like us. And because they have walked this road before us, they understand our struggles from the inside out. When I am wrestling with my anger, I don't have to explain it to Columba. He gets it. When I am afraid to answer God's call, I don't have to justify my fear to Patrick. He knows it. The saints are the ultimate proof that we are not alone in our struggles. They are the friends who can sit with us in our darkness without flinching, because they have been there too.

Their companionship is a powerful antidote to the shame and isolation that so often accompany our struggles.

3. They are Intercessors Who Pray for Us.

The saints are not just a silent cheering section; they are active participants in our lives. They are in the very presence of God, praying for us. The book of Revelation gives us this stunning image: "the twenty-four elders fell before the Lamb, each holding a harp, and golden bowls full of incense, which are the prayers of the saints" (Revelation 5:8). The prayers of the saints—both those on earth and those in heaven—are a sweet-smelling incense before the throne of God. To ask a saint to pray for us is to ask a member of our heavenly family to join their voice with ours.

We acknowledge that we are part of a body, a community of prayer that transcends death.

4. They are Proof That Transformation is Possible.

Perhaps most importantly, the saints are living proof that the Gospel is true. They are evidence that God can take the most broken, messed-up people and transform them into vessels of His grace. He can take a slave and make him an apostle. He can take a man consumed by anger and make him a founder of communities. He can take a woman on the margins of society and make her a spiritual mother to a nation. The saints are the finished products, the works of art that God has crafted out of the raw, messy material of human life. And in seeing them, we are given hope for our own transformation. If God could do it for them, He can do it for us.

Their lives are a resounding "Yes!" to the question that haunts us in our darkest moments: "Can I really be changed?"

Saints as Anam Cara

In my previous book, The Whisper of the Oak, we explored the beautiful Celtic concept of the anam cara, the soul friend. The anam cara is the person who knows your soul, the one with whom you can be completely yourself, without fear or pretence. It is a relationship of deep intimacy, honesty, and spiritual companionship. Finding an anam cara in this life is one of God's greatest gifts.

But what if this soul friendship is not limited by time and space? What if it is possible to have an anam cara who lived a thousand years ago? This is the radical and beautiful possibility that the communion of saints opens up to us. The saints can be our soul friends.

Think about what makes for a true soul friendship. It is a relationship of mutual knowing. Your anam cara sees you, truly sees you, in all your glory and all your brokenness, and loves you still. And you, in turn, see and love them. This is precisely the kind of relationship we can have with the saints. As we read their stories, as we learn about their struggles and their triumphs, we come to know them. We see their humanity, their passions, their unique way of loving God. We begin to feel a kinship, a friendship.

And in a way that is mysterious but no less real, they come to know us. As members of the body of Christ who are now perfected in heaven, they see with the eyes of Christ. They see us not just as we are, but as we are becoming. They know our potential, our calling, our deepest desires. They see the person God created us to be, even when we cannot see it ourselves. And they love that person. They cheer for that person. They pray for that person to come into being.

This is a soul friendship of a different order. It is a friendship not based on shared experiences in the here and now, but on a shared life in Christ that transcends it. It is a friendship characterised by profound honesty. We cannot hide from the saints. We cannot pretend to be something we are not. They have already seen it all, in their own lives and in the lives of countless others. We can come to them with our anger, our lust, our pride, our fear, and they will not be shocked. They will not turn away. They will nod, with the quiet compassion of those who know, and they will pray for us.

My relationship with St. Columba is among the most honest in my life. I can't pretend to be a patient, gentle man with him. He knows better. He sees the fire in my belly, the pride in my heart. And because he sees it and loves me anyway, I am free to be honest with myself about it. His companionship does not enable my sin; it exposes it, leading to repentance and healing. He is the soul friend who is not afraid to hold up a mirror to my soul, because he knows that the God who transformed him is at work changing me too.

This is the invitation of this chapter, and of this book. It is an invitation to expand your network. It is an invitation to discover that you have a family you never knew you had, a family of wise, compassionate, and fiercely loving soul friends who are waiting to walk with you, to pray for you, and to cheer you on as you run the race that is set before you.

Practices for This Chapter

1. Choose a Patron Saint: A patron saint is simply a saint with whom you feel a particular connection, one who you choose to be your primary companion and intercessor. Based on the brief introductions in this chapter, or on your own research, choose one Celtic saint to be your patron for the duration of this book. Don't overthink it. Who are you drawn to? Whose story resonates with your own? Choose one, and commit to getting to know them.

2. Read a Saint's Life: Find a biography or a collection of stories about your chosen patron saint and begin to read it. Don't read it like a history textbook. Read it like a letter from a friend. Pay attention to the parts of their story that make you feel something—inspiration, recognition, even irritation. Underline them. Journal about them. Begin getting to know this person.

3. Create a Sacred Space: You don't need an elaborate chapel to connect with the saints. Find a small corner of your home—a corner of your desk, a spot on your bookshelf, a windowsill—and make it a sacred space. Place an image of your patron saint there (you can find one online and print it out). Add a candle, a stone from your garden, a cross, anything that helps you to remember that this space is set apart for God. This will be the place where you meet with your heavenly friends. It is the first step in creating a thin place in your own home.

THE GREAT EXCHANGE: HOW THE SAINTS HELP US

One of the most beautiful aspects of the communion of saints is what theologians have sometimes called the "great exchange" or the "treasury of merit." These terms can sound a bit transactional, a bit like a spiritual bank account, and they have been the source of much misunderstanding and abuse in the history of the church. At its core, the idea is simple and profound. It is the idea that in the body of Christ, nothing is wasted. The good one member benefits the whole body. The prayers of one member lift all the others. The virtues of one member can, in a sense, be shared with those who lack them.

This is not a new or strange idea. We see it all the time in our human families. A mother's patience can create a space of peace for her whole family. A father's courage can inspire his children to be brave. A friend's generosity can ripple outwards, touching lives far beyond their immediate circle. In the same way, the virtues of the saints are not just for them; they are for us.

When we are struggling with impatience, we can ask St. Thérèse of Lisieux, the great teacher of the "little way," to share her patience with us.

When we are struggling with fear, we can ask St. Patrick to lend us his courage.

When we are struggling with anger, we can ask St. Columba to cover us with his hard-won self-control.

This is not a magical transaction. It is not as if the saints have a finite supply of virtue that they can dispense to us. Instead, it is that by connecting with them, by bringing our weakness into contact with their strength, we are drawn into the very life of Christ, who is the source of all virtue. The saints are the channels through which the grace of Christ flows to us in a particular and personal way. They are the elder brothers and sisters who have learned to draw deeply from the well of God's life, and they are eager to show us how to do the same.

I have experienced this great exchange in my own life in a powerful way. In the early days of my journey, I was a man of immense passion but very little discipline. I was prone to grand gestures and dramatic resolutions, but I had no staying power. I would start a new spiritual practice with great enthusiasm, only to abandon it a week later when the initial excitement wore off. I was like a spiritual sprinter, not a marathon runner. And I was constantly burning out.

In my reading, I encountered the stories of the desert fathers, the early Christian monks who withdrew to the wilderness to seek God in silence and solitude. I was drawn to their radical commitment, but I was also intimidated by their asceticism. One of the key practices of the desert fathers was the cultivation of apatheia, a Greek term often translated as "passionlessness" or "dispassion." For a long time, this word was a stumbling block for me. I was a passionate man. I didn't want to be passionless. It sounded boring, lifeless, grey.

But as I began to walk with the saints, particularly the Celtic saints, so influenced by the desert tradition, I came to understand that apatheia does not mean the absence of passion. It means the ordering of passion. It is the state of inner stillness and freedom that comes when our passions are no longer our masters, but our servants. It is the quiet, steady, unwavering focus on God that is not swayed by the shifting winds of emotion or circumstance. It is, in short, a spiritual discipline.

This was what I lacked. And so, I began to pray. I prayed to St. Anthony of the Desert, the father of monasticism. I prayed to St. Benedict, the great teacher of stability and order. I prayed to St. Columbanus, whose monastic rule was famously strict. "Brothers," I would pray, "you know what it is to live a disciplined life. You know what it is to order your passions for the love of God. I do not. Lend me your strength. Teach me your ways. Pray for me, that I might become a man of discipline, a man of stability, a man whose passion is channelled for the glory of God."

Slowly, almost imperceptibly at first, things began to change. I found the grace to stick with my morning prayer, even on the days when I didn't feel like it. I found the strength to fast, not just for a day, but week after week. I found the patience to sit in silence, even when my mind was racing. The change was not dramatic. It was the slow, steady, patient work of grace, flowing to me through the companionship and the prayers of my heavenly friends. They were sharing their strength with me. They were teaching me their discipline. They were drawing me into the ordered, passionate, disciplined life of Christ Himself.

This is the great exchange. It is the beautiful, mysterious way that we, as members of the body of Christ, can bear one another's burdens and share one another's gifts. It is the truth that in the family of God, your strength can meet my weakness, and my fullness can fill your emptiness. And it is a truth that extends across the thin veil of death, connecting us to the great treasury of grace that is stored up in the lives of the saints.

So, do not be afraid to ask. Do not be afraid to come to the saints with your emptiness, your weakness, your lack. They are not there to judge you. They are there to help you. They are there to share with you the gifts that God has given them, so that you, too, can become a gift to the world. This is the logic of grace. This is the economy of the kingdom. This is the communion of saints.

A Family of Misfits

I want to conclude this chapter with one final thought. The communion of saints is not a family of perfect, well-adjusted people. It is a family of misfits. It is a family of rebels and poets, of dreamers and fighters, of hermits and missionaries. It is a family of people who did not fit comfortably into the world because they lived in another.

Think of St. Francis of Assisi, who stripped naked in the town square to renounce his father's wealth. Think of St. Catherine of Siena, the uneducated dyer's daughter who fearlessly rebuked popes and princes. Think of St. Benedict Joseph Labre, the "holy hobo" who spent his life wandering the streets of Rome, living among the poor and the outcast. These were not normal people. They were strange. They were eccentric. They were on fire with the love of God, and it made them do strange and beautiful things.

And the Celtic saints are perhaps the most gloriously misfit family of all. They are a wild, passionate, earthy bunch. They are men like St. Columba, who wrestled with his temper. They are women such as St. Brigid, who defied the conventions of their time to build a community in which men and women lived and worked together. They are hermits like St. Kevin, who preferred the company of birds and animals to that of humans. They are pilgrims like St. Brendan, who set out on the open sea in a small leather boat, not knowing where he was going, but trusting that God would lead him.

This is our family. This is our heritage. And it is a profound comfort to me, as a man who has always felt like a misfit, to know that I belong to this family. I belong to a family of people who were not afraid to be different, who were not afraid to be strange, who were not afraid to be fully and gloriously themselves, because they knew that God beloved them.

So, if you have ever felt like you don't fit in, if you have ever felt like you are too much—too passionate, too sensitive, too angry, too strange—then I have good news for you. You are in the right place. You have found your family. The communion of saints is the home for all the holy misfits, all the glorious oddballs, all the passionate, broken, beautiful souls who have fallen in love with Jesus and have given their lives to Him without reservation.

Welcome home. You belong here. We have been waiting for you.

Chapter 3:

The Theology of Spiritual Companionship

My journey toward embracing the communion of saints was not linear. It was a wrestling match. For every step forward my heart took, my head took two steps back. The encounters I had with St. Patrick and St. Columba were undeniably real and life-changing, but the theologian in me—a theologian trained in a tradition deeply suspicious of anything that smacked of "popish superstition"—was in a constant state of alarm. I felt like a man caught in a spiritual tug-of-war. My experience was pulling me in one direction, while my theological training was yanking me in the other.

I remember one particularly intense conversation with my own anam cara, an older, wiser pastor named David, who had walked with me through the darkest days of my early transformation. We were sitting in his study, a room that smelled of old books and pipe tobacco, and I was pacing the floor, trying to articulate the war that was raging inside me.

"I don't understand it, David," I said, my voice tight with frustration. "I know what I experienced. I know that Columba was with me in that room. I know he helped me. But my mind keeps screaming that it's impossible. It's unbiblical. It's a slippery slope to idolatry. I feel like I'm betraying everything I've been taught, everything I believe about the sufficiency of Christ."

David listened patiently, his chin resting on his hand, his eyes full of a quiet, compassionate wisdom. He let me vent all my fears, all my objections, all my carefully constructed theological arguments. When I finally ran out of steam and slumped into a chair, he was silent for a long moment. Then he leaned forward and said, "Stuart, you're trying to fit an ocean into a teacup. Your experience of God has expanded, but your theological categories have remained the same. You don't need to abandon your theology. You need to expand it."

He then stood up, pulled a dusty, well-worn Bible from his shelf, and said, "Let's go back to the beginning. Let's look at the map the Scriptures give us. I think you'll find that this country you've stumbled into is not as foreign as you think. It's been there all along. You just haven't had the eyes to see it."

That conversation was a turning point for me. It was the beginning of a long, slow, and incredibly fruitful journey back into the Scriptures and the history of the church, a journey to find a theological home for my experience. It was a journey to bridge my heart and my head, to find a way to be both intellectually honest and experientially open. This chapter is the fruit of that journey. It is the map that David began to draw for me that day. I attempt to show you, as he showed me, that the communion of saints is not a strange, unbiblical innovation, but a deep, beautiful, and essential part of our Christian faith, rooted in the very heart of the Gospel.

BIBLICAL FOUNDATIONS: THE FAMILY ALBUM OF FAITH

For many Protestants, the first and most important question is, "Is it in the Bible?" It's a good question. Our faith is grounded in the Word of God, and any practice or doctrine, no matter how beautiful or compelling, must be tested against the witness of Scripture. For a long time, I believed that the Bible was silent on the communion of saints, or even hostile to it. But as David began to show me, the truth is that the Bible is saturated with this reality. It doesn't always use the phrase "communion of saints," but the concept is woven into the very fabric of the biblical narrative.

The story of the Bible is the story of God creating a family. From the call of Abraham to the formation of Israel, from the gathering of the disciples to the birth of the church, God is always at work, creating a people for Himself. And this family, these people, are not bound by blood or by geography, but by a covenant of grace, a shared life in God. The central miracle of the Gospel is that through Christ, we are adopted into this family. As the Apostle Paul writes, "So then you are no longer strangers and aliens, but you are fellow citizens with the saints and members of the household of God" (Ephesians 2:19).

This household, this family, is not limited to the people we can see and touch. It is a vast, sprawling, multi-generational family that includes all who have placed their faith in Christ, from the beginning of time until the end. This is the breathtaking vision of Hebrews 12, which we touched on in the first chapter. After recounting the long list of Old Testament heroes in chapter 11—the "family album" of our faith—the author declares, "Therefore, since we are surrounded by so great a cloud of witnesses..." (Hebrews 12:1). The image is of an athlete running a race in a massive stadium. The "cloud of witnesses" is the fans in the stands, the family members who have run the race before and are now cheering us on. They are not passive observers; they are active participants in our journey. Their presence is intended to encourage, inspire, and remind us that we are not alone.

But the Bible goes even further. It suggests that the saints in heaven are not just cheering for us; they are praying for us. In the book of Revelation, John is given a vision of the heavenly throne room. And what does he see? He sees the twenty-four elders, representing the people of God, falling down before the Lamb, "each holding a harp, and golden bowls full of incense, which are the prayers of the saints" (Revelation 5:8). Later, in chapter 8, he sees an angel at the altar, who "was given much incense to offer with the prayers of all the saints on the golden altar before the throne" (Revelation 8:3). The prayers of the saints—all the saints, both in heaven and on earth—are rising before God as a pleasing aroma. This is a stunning image. It suggests that prayer is a communal activity, a great chorus of praise and petition that unites the church across the veil of death. Those who have gone before us are not silent; they are praying. And their prayers are mingled with ours at the very throne of God.

This idea of a unified, praying church is central to Paul's theology of the body of Christ. In 1 Corinthians 12, he uses the powerful metaphor of a human body to describe the church. "For just as the body is one and has many members, and all the members of the body, though many, are one body, so it is with Christ" (1 Corinthians 12:12). In this body, every member is essential. Every member has a role to play.

The members are interconnected and interdependent. "If one member suffers, all suffer together; if one member is honoured, all rejoice together" (1 Corinthians 12:26). Paul is speaking here of the living, visible church on earth. But does this profound unity, this deep interconnectedness, cease to exist when a member of the body dies? Does death sever the body of Christ?

The consistent witness of the New Testament is a resounding "No!" In Christ, we are one body, and that unity is stronger than death. The saints in heaven are still members of the body. They are the "members who have been honoured," and they are rejoicing with us and suffering with us, praying for us and encouraging us.

This is the biblical foundation for the communion of saints. It is not based on a few obscure proof-texts, but on the grand, overarching story of the Bible: the story of God creating a family, the story of our adoption into that family through Christ, and the story of the unbreakable unity of that family in the body of Christ. The communion of saints is not an optional extra for the Christian life; it is the very air we breathe as members of God's household.

Historical Foundations: An Ancient and Honoured Practice

One of the things that gave me pause in my early journey was the feeling that this practice of connecting with the saints was a later invention, a medieval corruption of the pure, simple faith of the early church. But as I began to study the history of the church, I discovered that the opposite was true. The veneration of the saints and the belief in their ongoing intercession are among the most ancient and universal practices of the Christian faith.

The practice began with the martyrs. In the early centuries of the church, to be a Christian was often a death sentence. Christians were persecuted, arrested, tortured, and killed for their faith. These martyrs were regarded as the ultimate heroes of the faith, those who had followed Christ even to the point of death. The living would gather the remains of the martyrs, bury them with honour, and then meet at their tombs on the anniversary of their death to celebrate the Eucharist and remember their witness. These were not morbid, gloomy occasions. They were celebrations of victory. The martyrs were not seen as dead, but as having entered into the fullness of life. They were the victors who had finished the race, and the living gathered to honour them and to draw strength from their example.

Very quickly, this practice of honouring the martyrs grew into asking for their prayers. In the catacombs of Rome, the underground burial places of the early Christians, we find graffiti scrawled on the walls of the tombs, simple prayers like, "Paul and Peter, pray for Victor." These were not formal, liturgical prayers. These were the spontaneous, heartfelt cries of ordinary Christians who believed that their martyred brothers and sisters were in the presence of God and could pray for them. They believed that the martyrs, who had shown such great love and courage on earth, would not cease to love and care for them in heaven.

As the age of martyrdom passed, this practice was extended to include not only martyrs but also "confessors"—those who had lived lives of heroic virtue and had confessed the faith with their lives, if not with their deaths. These were the great bishops and theologians, the desert fathers and mothers, the holy men and women whose lives shone with the light of Christ. Their stories were told and retold, their writings were read and cherished, and they were looked to as spiritual guides and intercessors.

By the fourth century, the practice of venerating the saints and asking for their prayers was a universal and unquestioned part of Christian life and worship, in both the East and the West. The great theologians of the church—Augustine, Jerome, Basil the Great, Gregory of Nyssa—all wrote about it and encouraged it. For them, it was neither a strange nor a dangerous innovation. It was a natural expression of their belief in the unity of the body of Christ.

This is the tradition that the Celtic Christians inherited. When St. Patrick brought Christianity to Ireland in the fifth century, he brought with him this deep, ancient belief in the communion of saints. But the Celts, with their unique worldview, gave it a distinct flavour. For them, the saints were not just heavenly intercessors; they were earthly companions. They were woven into the landscape, into the seasons, into the daily rhythms of life. They were the patrons of wells and mountains, the guardians of tribes and families. They were the anam cara of the whole people. The line between the church on earth (the church militant) and the church in heaven (the church triumphant) was almost non-existent. They were simply one church, one family, one communion, living and praying together in the presence of God.

So, when we practice the communion of saints today, we are not engaging in a medieval superstition or a Catholic invention. We are stepping into a stream of practice that is as old as the church itself. We are joining our voices to a chorus of prayer that has been rising to the throne of God for two thousand years. We are recovering a lost part of our own family heritage.

Theological Foundations: Unpacking the Mystery

Even with a solid biblical and historical foundation, the communion of saints can still feel theologically puzzling. How does it actually work? How can the dead hear us? How does this not interfere with Christ's unique role as mediator? These are essential questions, and they deserve thoughtful answers. As my friend David said, we don't need to abandon our theology; we need to expand it. We need to stretch our minds to embrace a mystery that is larger than our neat, tidy categories.

At the heart of this mystery are two profound Christian truths: the nature of time and the nature of the body of Christ.

First, the nature of time. We experience time as a linear progression: past, present, future. But God does not. God is eternal. He lives outside of time. For Him, all of time is present at once. This is a concept that is counterintuitive, but it has profound implications for our understanding of the communion of saints. Those who have died in Christ have not ceased to exist; they have entered into God's eternal now. They are, in a sense, more present to us than our friends who live across the country, because they are present in the same eternal moment in which we are living our temporal lives. The barrier between us is not one of time or space, but of perception. They are in the same room, but in a different dimension. And because they are in Christ, and we are in Christ, that dimensional barrier is permeable.

Second, the nature of the body of Christ. As we have seen, the New Testament is emphatic that the church is one body, united in Christ. This is not just a nice metaphor; it is a spiritual reality. Through our baptism, we are mystically united with Christ and with all who are in Him. This union is so profound that Paul can say, "It is no longer I who live, but Christ who lives in me" (Galatians 2:20). If Christ lives in me. Christ lives in St. Patrick, then I am united with St. Patrick in a way that is more real and more intimate than my union with my own earthly family. We are members of the same body, animated by the same Spirit, sharing the same life. Death cannot sever this bond. As the old saying goes, "We are all one in Christ, and Christ is not divided."

When we put these two truths together—the eternal nature of God's presence and the mystical unity of the body of Christ—the communion of saints begins to make a profound kind of sense. It is not about the dead hearing us through some spiritualistic telephone. It is about us, as members of the same body, living in the same eternal presence of God, communicating with one another through our shared life in Christ. Our prayers to the saints are not shouted across a vast, empty chasm. They are whispered in the heart of Christ, where all the members of His body are present and united.

This brings us to the crucial question of Christ's unique role as mediator. The fear that praying to the saints diminishes Christ is perhaps the most significant stumbling block for many Protestants. And it is a fear that must be taken seriously. The New Testament is obvious that Jesus is the one and only mediator between God and humanity. He is the way, the truth, and the life. No one comes to the Father except through Him. So, how do we reconcile this with the practice of asking the saints to pray for us?

The key is to distinguish between mediation and intercession. Christ is the one mediator of our salvation. His death on the cross is the one, all-sufficient sacrifice for our sins. He is the one who has bridged the gap between a holy God and sinful humanity. Nothing and no one can be added to His finished work. But intercession—praying for one another—is not a work of mediation; it is a work of participation. It is one of the primary ways that we, as members of Christ's body, participate in His ongoing life and ministry. When we pray for one another, we are not acting as independent mediators. We are joining our voices to the great prayer of Christ Himself, who "is at the right hand of God, who indeed is interceding for us" (Romans 8:34).

The saints in heaven are doing the same thing. They are not a rival team of mediators. They are members of our team, our family, who are joining their prayers with ours, all offered to the Father through the one mediator, Jesus Christ. To ask for their prayers is not to bypass Christ; it is to embrace the reality of His body more fully. We acknowledge that we are not meant to be spiritual individualists but members of a vast, praying family. The saints do not stand between Christ and us; they stand with us before Christ.

My own journey to understand this was slow. It required me to let go of my fiercely independent, "just me and Jesus" spirituality and to embrace the messy, beautiful, communal reality of the church. It required me to be humble enough to admit that I need help, not just from God, but from my brothers and sisters, both on earth and in heaven. And it required me to trust that the body of Christ is a real thing, a living organism, a mystical union that is stronger than my doubts, stronger than my fears, and even stronger than death itself.

The Cruciform Life and the Communion of Saints

In The Whisper of the Oak, we examined the concept of the cruciform life—the life shaped by the cross of Christ. It is a life of dying and rising, of letting go of our own ego and ambition, and of finding our true life in self-giving love. The communion of saints is the ultimate expression of this cruciform life. It is the community that is formed at the foot of the cross.

The cross is the great meeting place. It is the place where a holy God and sinful humanity are reconciled. It is the place where Jew and Gentile, slave and free, male and female are made one in Christ. And it is the place where the church on earth and the church in heaven are united. The cross is the bridge that spans the chasm of death. It is the tree of life whose branches reach from earth to heaven, and all the members of God's family find their home in its shade.

To live the cruciform life is to die to our radical individualism, our proud self-sufficiency, our fear of vulnerability. It is to die to the illusion that we can make it on our own. And it is to rise to a new life of communion, of interdependence, of shared life in the body of Christ. Walking with the saints is a profound way to live out this dying-and-rising. When we ask a saint for help, we are dying to our pride. We acknowledge that we are insufficient. When we receive their companionship and prayers, we are recognising that we are part of something larger than ourselves, held and supported by a love wider and deeper than we can imagine.

My own story is a testament to this. The man I used to be was a radical individualist. I trusted no one. I relied on no one. My life was a constant, violent struggle for survival. When I came to faith, I transferred that individualism to my spiritual life. It was me and Jesus against the world. But the cross kept getting in the way. The cross kept reminding me that I was not saved alone, but saved into a family. The cross kept inviting me to lay down my arms, to let go of my self-sufficiency, and to find my life not in fighting, but in belonging.

Walking with the saints has been a school of the cruciform life for me. They have taught me what it means to be a son, a brother, a member of a family. They have taught me that true strength lies not in independence but in interdependence. They have taught me that the goal of the Christian life is not to become a spiritual superhero, but to become a humble, loving member of the body of Christ. They have taught me, in short, what it means to live a life shaped by the cross.

Practices for This Chapter

1. Theological Journaling: This chapter has covered some deep theological ground. Take some time this week to journal about your own theological journey. What were you taught about the saints growing up? What are your fears or hesitations? What questions are still lingering in your mind? Be honest. Write them all down. Then, offer them to God in prayer. Ask Him to lead you into a deeper understanding of this beautiful truth.

2. Discuss with an Anam Cara: If you have a soul friend or a spiritual community, share this chapter with them. Discuss your questions and your discoveries. The theology of the communion of saints is best understood not in isolation, but in community. Listen to the perspectives of others. Wrestle with the Scriptures together. Pray for one another as you seek to grow in your understanding.

3. Pray the Creed: Many of us have recited the Apostles' Creed countless times without much thought. This week, I invite you to pray it slowly, meditatively. When you reach the line "I believe in the communion of saints," pause. Sit with those words. What do they mean to you now? What would it look like for you to truly live as if you believe them? Ask God to make this line of the creed not just a doctrine you affirm, but a reality you experience.

The Great Cloud of Witnesses: A Deeper Dive into Hebrews 12

Let us return for a moment to that magnificent image in Hebrews 12: "Therefore, since we are surrounded by so great a cloud of witnesses…" This is perhaps the most important biblical passage for understanding the communion of saints, and it warrants further analysis.

The author has just spent an entire chapter—the great "Hall of Faith" of Hebrews 11—recounting the stories of the Old Testament saints. He has painted a vivid picture of our spiritual ancestry, a long line of men and women who lived and died by faith, often in the face of incredible hardship and opposition. They are our family. They are our heritage. And now, in chapter 12, he brings them into the present. They are not just historical figures; they are a "great cloud of witnesses" who are surrounding us, right now, as we run our own race.

What does it mean to be a "witness"? The Greek word is *martys*, from which we get our English word *"martyr."* A witness is someone who testifies to the truth of what they have seen and experienced. The saints in this great cloud are witnesses in at least three ways.

First, they are witnesses to God's faithfulness. Their lives are a testament to God's trustworthiness. They faced famine and flood, exile and execution, and through it all, they held on to the promise of God. They are the proof that God is faithful to His people, that He will never leave us or forsake us. When we are tempted to doubt God's goodness, when we feel that our own struggles are too great to bear, we can look to this great cloud of witnesses and take courage. They are saying to us, "We have been there. We have faced the fire. And God was faithful. He will be faithful to you, too."

Second, they are witnesses to the reality of the unseen world. The author of Hebrews defines faith as "the assurance of things hoped for, the conviction of things not seen" (Hebrews 11:1). The saints are those who lived their lives on the basis of this conviction. They saw the invisible kingdom of God, and they ordered their lives around it. They "endured as seeing him who is invisible" (Hebrews 11:27). In a world that is obsessed with the material, the visible, the quantifiable, the saints are a powerful witness to the reality of the spiritual world. They remind us that what we see is not all there is. They invite us to lift our eyes from the mud and the mire of our daily struggles and to fix them on the eternal realities of God's kingdom. They are the proof that the unseen world is more real, more solid, more lasting than the fleeting world we see around us.

Third, and perhaps most profoundly, they are witnesses to us. They are watching us. They are aware of our race, our struggle, our journey. This is a staggering thought. We are not running in an empty stadium. A vast, loving, and attentive audience surrounds us. They are not there to judge us or to criticise our form. They are there to support us. They are the ultimate fan club, the Heavenly Cheering section, the family that is passionately invested in our success.

Imagine running a marathon. Your legs are burning, your lungs are screaming, and you feel like you can't take another step. And then, you hear your name being shouted from the crowd. You look up, and you see the faces of your family, your friends, your loved ones. They are smiling, waving, shouting your name. What does that do to you? It gives you a new surge of energy. It reminds you why you are running. It connects you to a love that is larger than your pain. This is the gift of the great cloud of witnesses. They are our heavenly family, shouting our names, reminding us that we are loved, that we are not alone, and that the finish line is worth the struggle.

My friend David once put it to me this way. He said, "Stuart, when you were a young man, you were a fighter. You lived for the roar of the crowd. You fed on their energy. You fought harder because you knew they were watching. What if the Christian life is the same? What if God has given us a crowd, a heavenly crowd, to cheer us on, to give us strength, to remind us that this fight is not just for us, but for the glory of the One who has called us into the ring?"

That image has stayed with me. I am still a fighter. However, I am now fighting a different battle. I am fighting for holiness, for love, for the kingdom of God. And I am not fighting alone. I am fighting in a stadium that is packed to the rafters with the greatest champions of all time. And they are on my side. They are in my corner. They are shouting my name. How can I give up, when I am surrounded by so great a cloud of witnesses?

THE BODY OF CHRIST: MORE THAN A METAPHOR

Let us examine Paul's metaphor of the body of Christ in greater detail. This is not just one metaphor among many; it is his primary way of describing the church. It is a metaphor that is rich in implications for our understanding of the communion of saints.

In a body, every member is unique and essential. The eye cannot say to the hand, "I have no need of you," nor again the head to the feet, "I have no need of you" (1 Corinthians 12:21). There is a radical equality and a radical interdependence in the body of Christ. We need each other. We are designed to function together.

In a body, there is a shared life. The same life force, the same breath, the same heartbeat animate all the members. In the body of Christ, that life force is the Holy Spirit. We are all partakers of the same Spirit, and it is this shared Spirit that makes us one.

In a body, there is a profound sympathy between the members. "If one member suffers, all suffer together; if one member is honoured, all rejoice together" (1 Corinthians 12:26). There is a mysterious, organic connection that binds us together, so that the joy of one becomes the joy of all. The pain of one becomes the pain of all.

Now, here is the crucial question: Does this profound, organic, Spirit-filled unity cease to exist when a member of the body dies? Is the body of Christ a temporary, earthly organisation, or is it an eternal, spiritual organism?

The New Testament witness is clear. The body of Christ is an infinite reality. Those who have died in Christ are not ex-members of the body; they are members in good standing, members who have been promoted, members who are now participating in the life of the body in a new and more profound way.

If this is true, then the implications are staggering. It means the body's interdependence is not limited by death. We still need the saints in heaven, and in a way, they still need us. We need their wisdom, their prayers, their example. And they, in their love for us, need our faithfulness, our perseverance, our growth in holiness, so that the body as a whole can be built up in love.

It means that the shared life of the body is not limited by death. The same Holy Spirit continues to animate us. The same Spirit that filled St. Patrick with courage and St. Brigid with generosity is at work in us today. And we can draw on that shared life, that shared reservoir of grace, through our connection with them.

And it means that the profound sympathy of the body is not limited by death. The saints in heaven are not indifferent to our suffering. They are not detached from our struggles. "If one member suffers, all suffer together." They suffer with us, they grieve with us, they long for our healing and our wholeness. And they rejoice with us. Every small victory, every step of faith, every act of love sends a ripple of joy throughout the entire body, both in heaven and on earth.

This is not just a beautiful idea. It is a reality that can transform our experience of the Christian life. It means that we are never alone in our suffering. We are held in the compassionate embrace of a vast family that suffers with us. It means that our small, feeble efforts at holiness are not insignificant. They are part of a great, cosmic project, the building up of the body of Christ, and they are a source of joy to the saints in heaven. And it means that we have access to a vast reservoir of wisdom, strength, and prayer, the collective spiritual capital of the entire family of God.

My journey from a violent, isolated individualist to a member of this great family has been the central journey of my life. It has been a journey of learning to receive, to be dependent, to be loved. And it has been a journey of learning to see myself not as a lone warrior, but as a humble, grateful member of the most beautiful, most powerful, most loving body in the universe: the body of Christ.

Chapter 4:

Prayer and Invocation: Speaking with the Saints

I had the theology straight in my head. I understood, at least intellectually, that the communion of saints was a biblical, historical, and theologically sound reality. I had chosen my patron saint—St. Columba, my fellow hothead—and I had even set up a small, sacred space on my bookshelf with a printed icon of him, a smooth stone from a nearby river, and a candle. I was ready. It was time to pray.

And I was terrified.

It felt utterly, profoundly awkward. I sat in my chair, staring at the flickering candle, my hands sweating. What was I supposed to say? How did this even work? I felt like a teenage boy trying to make a phone call to a girl he had a crush on, my mind a complete blank, my heart pounding in my chest. All my carefully constructed theology evaporated in a cloud of self-consciousness.

I decided to try a formal approach. I cleared my throat. "O glorious St. Columba," I began, my voice sounding strange and stilted in the quiet room. "Thou who art a prince of the Church and a beacon of light in the darkness…" I trailed off. It felt ridiculous. I was performing. I was trying to sound "holy," and it was falling completely flat. This wasn't prayer; it was a bad audition for a medieval play.

I tried a different tack. Maybe I was supposed to be more direct. "St. Columba," I said, trying to sound casual, "I'm Stuart. Nice to meet you. I'm the guy with the anger problem. You too, I hear. So, uh… any tips?" Again, silence. The only response was the flickering of the candle, which seemed to be mocking my foolishness.

I slumped back in my chair, defeated. This was a mistake. It was weird. It was a spiritual dead end. I was about to blow out the candle and put the icon in a drawer when a memory surfaced. It was a memory of my early days of sobriety, of sitting in a circle of other broken men, and of the raw, desperate honesty of those conversations. We didn't use fancy language. We didn't try to impress each other. We just told the truth. We said, "I'm struggling. I'm scared. I need help."

What if that was the key? What if I stopped trying to perform for Columba and just told him the truth?

I took a deep breath. I closed my eyes. And I spoke from the heart. "Columba," I whispered, the name no longer feeling strange on my lips. "I'm a mess. I'm so angry all the time. It feels like a wild animal is living inside me, and I'm afraid it's going to break loose and destroy everything I love. You know what this is like. You lived with this beast. You fought this fight. I don't know how to do it. Please, brother. Pray for me. Show me the way."

I sat there in the silence, tears streaming down my face. And in that silence, something shifted. There was no booming voice from heaven. No vision of a Celtic monk appeared before me. But there was a profound sense of… companionship. A sense of not being alone in my struggle. It was a quiet, steady, reassuring presence, a feeling of being seen and understood by someone who had been there before. It was the feeling of a hand on my shoulder, the silent nod of a fellow warrior who knew the cost of this particular battle.

That was my first real prayer to a saint. It wasn't eloquent. It wasn't theological. It was raw, honest, and desperate. And it was the beginning of a conversation that has continued to this day, a conversation that has saved my life more times than I can count. In this chapter, we will explore how to have that conversation.

We will move from the theology of the communion of saints to its practice.

We will learn how to speak with the saints, not as distant, marble figures, but as living, present, and deeply compassionate friends.

The Heart of the Matter: Conversation, Not Worship

Before we go any further, we must be absolutely clear about one thing: praying to the saints is not the same as worshipping them. This is the single greatest point of confusion and fear for those coming from a Protestant background, and we must address it head-on. Worship belongs to God alone. God is the Creator; we are the creatures. He is the source of all life, all goodness, all grace. To give the worship that is due to God to any created being, whether on earth or in heaven, is the very definition of idolatry.

So, what are we doing when we pray to the saints? We are not worshipping them. We are talking to them. We are having a conversation with them. We are treating them as what they are: our elder brothers and sisters, our fellow members of the body of Christ who have finished the race and are now in the presence of God. It is the difference between kneeling before a king in adoration and sitting down with a trusted friend for a cup of coffee.

When I pray to God the Father, I am coming before the sovereign Lord of the universe. I am approaching the throne of grace with awe and reverence. I am worshipping the One who spoke the galaxies into being. When I pray to Jesus, I am speaking with my Lord and my Saviour, the one who died for my sins and rose again for my salvation. When I pray to the Holy Spirit, I am communing with the very breath of God who dwells within me.

When I pray to St. Columba, I am talking to a brother who knows what it's like to have a temper. I am asking for the prayers of a friend who has walked this road before me. I am seeking the wisdom of an elder who has learned a few things about following Jesus in a broken world. My posture is different. My language is different. My intention is different.

Think of it this way. If you were struggling with a particular sin, you might go to your pastor or your anam cara and say, "I'm really struggling with this. Will you pray for me?" You are not worshipping your pastor. You are not treating your anam cara as a mediator of salvation. You are simply asking a member of your earthly family to support you in prayer. Praying to the saints is the same thing. It is simply extending that request to our heavenly family. It is asking St. Patrick to pray for us, just as we would ask our friend Patrick down the street to pray for us. The only difference is that St. Patrick has a much better view of the throne room.

This distinction is crucial. If at any point your prayer to a saint begins to feel like worship, if you find yourself giving them the adoration and the ultimate trust that belongs to God alone, then you must stop. You must recalibrate. You must return to the simple, humble posture of a younger sibling asking an older sibling for help. The saints are not the destination; they are the signposts. They are not the light; they are the windows through which the light shines. And they are all, always, pointing us back to the one true Light, the one true Mediator, the one true object of our worship: Jesus Christ.

Four Ways to Speak with the Saints

Once we are clear that we are having a conversation, not offering worship, we can begin to explore the different forms that this conversation can take. Just as our discussions with our earthly friends vary depending on the situation, so too our conversations with our heavenly friends will have different flavours and textures. I have found it helpful to think of four primary ways of speaking with the saints: Conversation, Intercession, Invocation, and Gratitude.

1. Conversation (Speaking to): This is the most basic and, in many ways, the most profound form of prayer with the saints. It is the simple act of sharing your life with them. It is talking to them about your day, your joys, your sorrows, your struggles. It is treating them as a constant, present companion. This is the kind of prayer that I have with St. Columba. It is an ongoing dialogue. When I feel that familiar spark of anger, I will often whisper, "Columba, you see this? It's happening again. Be with me." When I manage to hold my tongue or walk away from a conflict, I will say, "Thanks, brother. We did it." It is a friendship. It is a shared life.

This kind of conversational prayer requires a particular kind of faith. It requires us to believe that the saints are truly present, truly listening, and truly care about the mundane details of our lives. It requires us to set aside our self-consciousness and speak with the simple, unvarnished honesty of a child speaking to a beloved family member. It may feel strange at first, but as you persevere, you will find that it becomes one of the most natural and comforting practices in your spiritual life. You will begin to experience the truth that you are never truly alone.

2. Intercession (Asking for): This is perhaps the most common and well-known form of prayer to the saints. It is the act of asking them to pray for us for a specific need. Just as we would ask our friends in our small group to pray for a job interview or a medical procedure, so we can ask the saints in heaven to join their prayers with ours. The saints have a particular power in their prayer because they are in the very presence of God. They see with a clarity that we do not have, and they pray with a purity of heart that we are still striving for. Their prayers are, as St. James says, "powerful and effective" (James 5:16).

We can ask for their prayers for anything, big or small. But it is particularly powerful to ask for the prayers of a saint who has a particular connection to our need. If you are struggling with addiction, you might ask for the prayers of St. Matt Talbot, the patron saint of alcoholics. If you are a writer struggling with writer's block, you might ask for the prayers of St. Francis de Sales, the patron saint of writers. If you are a teacher working with a difficult class, you might ask for the prayers of St. John Baptist de la Salle, the patron saint of teachers. This is not because the saints have specialised, magical powers. It is because they understand our struggle from the inside out. They have been there. They get it. And their prayers for us are filled with a particular empathy and compassion.

I do this all the time. Before I sit down to write, I often say a quick prayer: "St. Columba, you were a poet and a scribe. You loved the beauty of words. Pray for me, that my words might be true and beautiful, and that they might lead people to Christ." Before I give a talk or a sermon, I pray: "St. Patrick, you were a powerful preacher of the Gospel. You were not afraid to speak the truth in love. Pray for me, that I might have your courage and your clarity." This practice has transformed my work. It has turned it from a solitary, stressful performance into a collaborative, prayer-filled ministry.

3. Invocation (Calling upon): Invocation is a more urgent, in-the-moment form of prayer. It is the act of calling upon a saint's name in a moment of crisis, temptation, or need. It is a spiritual SOS, a cry for help from the front lines of the battle. When the temptation to anger is overwhelming, when the pull of an old addiction is almost irresistible, when the darkness of despair is closing in, we can call upon the name of a saint who has fought that same battle and won. "St. Columba, help me!" "St. Mary of Egypt, pray for me!" "St. Michael the Archangel, defend me!"

This is not a magic spell. The name of the saint has no power in itself. The power is in the act of turning away from the temptation and toward the communion of saints. It is the act of acknowledging our weakness and seeking help. It is the act of grabbing the hand of an elder brother or sister who is reaching out to us from the heavenly stands. In that moment of invocation, we are reminded that we are not alone in the fight. We are surrounded by a great cloud of witnesses, a heavenly army that is fighting with us and for us.

I have found this practice to be incredibly powerful in my own struggle with anger. That old, violent instinct can rise up so quickly, so powerfully, that I don't have time for a long, eloquent prayer. All I have time for is a desperate cry: "Columba!" And in that one word, I am doing so much. I am acknowledging my weakness. I am remembering his struggle. I am asking for his help. I choose to stand with the saints rather than with my sin. And time and time again, that simple, desperate cry has been enough to break the spell of my rage and to give me the grace to choose a different path.

4. Gratitude (Giving thanks for): Finally, our conversation with the saints should not be all about us and our needs. It should also be filled with gratitude. We should take the time to thank the saints for their prayers, companionship, and example. When a prayer is answered, when a temptation is overcome, when a moment of unexpected grace breaks through, we should turn to our heavenly friends and say, "Thank you."

This practice of gratitude does two things. First, it honours the saints and acknowledges their role in our lives. It treats them as true friends, not just as spiritual vending machines. Second, it trains our own hearts to see the work of God in our lives. When we are constantly looking for reasons to be grateful, we begin to notice the small, subtle ways God answers our prayers and provides for our needs. Our lives become a treasure hunt for grace, and we find it everywhere.

I have a practice of ending my day by thanking the saints who have walked with me. "Thank you, Patrick, for your courage today. Thank you, Brigid, for that opportunity to show hospitality. Thank you, Columba, for helping me hold my tongue in that meeting." This simple practice has reframed my entire day. It has helped me to see my life not as a series of random events, but as a shared journey, a collaborative project, a dance of grace between heaven and earth.

A Simple, Four-Step Guide to Prayer

Knowing the different types of prayer is helpful, but how do we actually do it? How do we move from theory to practice? Here is a simple, four-step process that you can use to guide your time of prayer with the saints. It is not a rigid formula, but a gentle framework, a set of training wheels to help you get started.

Step 1: Be Still. Identify your sacred space, the one we discussed in the last chapter. Light your candle. Take a few deep breaths. Let go of the noise and the hurry of your day. Offer this time to God. Ask the Holy Spirit to be present with you, to guide your prayer, and to open your heart to the companionship of the saints. You cannot have a deep conversation in a noisy, crowded room. The first step is always to cultivate inner and outer stillness.

Step 2: Remember. Call to mind the saint you have chosen to pray with. Look at their icon. Say their name. And then, remember their story. Remember who they were. Remember their struggles. Remember their virtues. Remember the ways that God worked in their life. You might even read a short passage from their biography or one of their writings. The goal of this step is to make the saint real to you. You are not praying to an abstract concept or a historical figure. You are praying to a person, a friend, a fellow traveller. Before you speak to them, take a moment to remember who they are.

Step 3: Speak. This is the heart of the prayer. Speak to the saint as you would a trusted friend. Be honest. Be vulnerable. Be yourself. You can use one of the four forms of prayer we just discussed. You can have a conversation and share your heart with them. You can ask for their intercession for a specific need. You can invoke their help in a moment of struggle. You can offer your gratitude for their presence in your life. Don't worry about getting the words right. Just speak from the heart. Tell them the truth. That is all that is required.

Step 4: Listen. Prayer is a two-way conversation. After you have spoken, take some time to be silent and to listen. This is often the most challenging step for us because we are accustomed to noise and activity. But it is essential. How do the saints speak to us? They do not usually speak in an audible voice. They speak in the quiet language of the heart. They speak through a sudden insight, a new perspective, a sense of peace, a feeling of courage. They speak through a passage of Scripture that comes to mind, or a memory that surfaces. They speak through the circumstances of our lives, the people we meet, and the opportunities that arise. Listening is an act of paying attention. It is an act of opening ourselves to the subtle, gentle, and often surprising ways that God and His saints are present and active in our lives.

That's it. Be still. Remember. Speak. Listen. This is a practice that you can do in five minutes or in an hour. It is a practice that will, over time, transform your relationship with the saints from a theological concept into a living, breathing friendship.

COMMON QUESTIONS AND CONCERNS

Even with this simple guide, you may still have questions and concerns. That's normal. This is a new and unfamiliar practice for many of us. Let's address a few of the most common ones.

"What if I feel silly?" You will. I did. It is a strange thing to talk to someone you can't see.

Acknowledge the feeling of silliness. Smile at it. And then, do it anyway. The sense of awkwardness will pass as the practice becomes more familiar and you begin to experience its fruits. Remember, you are not performing for anyone. You are having a private conversation with a friend. It's okay if it feels a little strange at first.

"What if I don't hear anything?" You probably won't, at least not in the way you expect.

The saints do not usually speak in a booming voice. Their communication is much more subtle. The key is to broaden your definition of "listening." Don't just listen for a voice in your head. Listen for a shift in your heart. Listen for a new idea. Listen for a sense of peace. Listen for the ways that God is moving in your life in the hours and days after your prayer. The saints are like master gardeners; they often plant seeds that do not sprout for a long time. Be patient. Trust the process. And keep listening.

"Am I doing it right?" If you are being honest, humble, and your ultimate focus is on Jesus, then you are doing it right.

There is no magic formula, no secret handshake. This is about a relationship, not a ritual. The only way to do it wrong is to turn it into a form of idolatry, to give the saint the worship that belongs to God alone. As long as you are honouring the saints as your elder brothers and sisters and worshipping God as your sovereign Lord, you are on the right path.

Practices for This Chapter

1. Daily Conversation: Commit to having a short, daily conversation with your patron saint. It doesn't have to be long or formal. Just a simple "Good morning," a quick sharing of your plans for the day, a desperate "Help!" in a moment of temptation, a grateful "Thank you" at the end of the day. Weave this conversation into the fabric of your daily life.

2. Pray a Litany: A litany is a form of prayer that consists of a series of petitions. The Litany of the Saints is an ancient and beautiful prayer that invokes the blessings of a long list of saints. You can find many versions of it online. This week, find one and pray it. As you pray the names of these saints, remember that you are part of a vast, praying family.

3. Write a Letter: Sometimes, it is easier to write than to speak. Take some time this week to write a letter to your patron saint. Tell them your story. Share your struggles. Ask your questions. Pour out your heart on the page. This can be a powerful way to clarify your thoughts and to deepen your sense of connection.

The Celtic Way of Prayer: A Deeper Dive

The Celtic Christians had an excellent and earthy way of praying with their saints. Their prayers were not abstract or theological; they were woven into the very fabric of their daily lives. They had prayers for milking the cow, lighting the fire, going to sleep, and waking up. And in all of these prayers, the saints were present as companions and protectors. This practice of constant, conversational prayer is one of the greatest gifts of the Celtic tradition to the wider church.

One of the most famous collections of these prayers is the Carmina Gadelica, a collection of hymns and incantations gathered in the Highlands and Islands of Scotland by Alexander Carmichael in the 19th century. While the collection is not without its scholarly controversies, it offers a striking glimpse into a world in which the saints were a constant, living presence. In these prayers, we see a seamless blending of the natural and the supernatural, the earthly and the heavenly.

A woman milking her cow might pray:

"The milking of the Fawn, of the brown cow, on the pasture of the plain, with the aid of Brigit the gentle, and of Mary the loving."

A man lighting his fire in the morning might pray:

"I will kindle my fire this morning in the presence of the holy angels of heaven, in the presence of Ariel of the loveliest form, in the presence of Uriel of the myriad charms, without malice, without jealousy, without envy, without fear, without terror of anyone under the sun, but the Holy Son of God to shield me."

What is so striking about these prayers is their intimacy and their immediacy. The saints are not distant figures; they are right there, in the byre, at the hearth. They are helpers, protectors, and friends. This is the heart of the Celtic way of prayer. It is not a separate, compartmentalised activity, but a constant, ongoing conversation with the entire family of God.

This is a practice that we can cultivate in our own lives. We can begin to weave the names of our patron saints into the prayers of our daily lives. When you are driving to work, you might say, "St. Brendan, you were a great navigator. Guide me safely on my journey today." When you are cooking a meal for your family, you might say, "St. Brigid, you were a woman of great hospitality. Bless this food and this family." When you are tucking your children into bed, you might say, "St. Kevin, you loved all of God's creatures. Watch over my little ones as they sleep."

This practice does something profound. It sanctifies the ordinary. It turns the mundane tasks of our daily lives into opportunities for prayer and communion. It reminds us that we are never alone, that even in the most routine moments of our day, we are surrounded by a great cloud of witnesses who love us, pray for us, and walk with us. It is a way of living in a thin place, a way of experiencing the nearness of heaven in the midst of our earthly lives.

The Power of Place: Praying with Saints in Their Sacred Sites

The Celtic Christians also had a strong sense of the power of place. They believed that certain places were "thin," places where the veil between heaven and earth was particularly transparent. These were often places of outstanding natural beauty—a holy well, a sacred mountain, a remote island—but they were also places that the prayers and the presence of a saint had hallowed. The saints had left a spiritual residue, an echo of their holiness, in the places where they had lived and prayed. And to go to these places was to enter into their story, to connect with their spirit, to feel their presence compellingly.

This is the origin of the great Celtic tradition of pilgrimage. To go on pilgrimage was to take a journey to a holy place, to a place where a saint had lived or died, to seek their prayers and to draw strength from their example. It was a physical journey that mirrored the soul's inner journey. It was a practice open to everyone, from kings to peasants.

We can still participate in this practice today. We can make a pilgrimage to Iona, the island of St. Columba. We can visit Glendalough, the valley of St. Kevin. We can climb Croagh Patrick, the holy mountain of St. Patrick. To go to these places is to step into a story that is still unfolding. It is to feel the prayers of centuries soaking into the very soil. It is to connect with our spiritual ancestors in a tangible, embodied way.

But we don't have to travel to Ireland or Scotland to experience the power of place. We can create our own sacred sites, our own thin places, right where we are. The sacred space we create in our home is a start. But we can also find places in our local area that feel thin to us. It might be a particular corner of a park, a bench by a river, or an old, beautiful church. We can consecrate these places with our own prayers. We can invite our patron saints to meet us there. We can make them our own personal pilgrimage sites.

I have a place like this. It is a small, hidden grove of oak trees in a park near my home. It is the place where I go when I need to be still, when I need to listen, when I need to feel the presence of God and His saints. I call it my "little Iona." And when I am there, I feel a deep connection to St. Columba, the man who found his own place of exile and transformation on a remote

Scottish island. I am not on Iona, but the spirit of Iona is with me. The companionship of Columba is with me. And in that small, ordinary grove of trees, the veil between heaven and earth becomes very thin indeed.

A Word of Encouragement

I want to end this chapter with a word of encouragement. This practice of praying with the saints may be new to you. It may feel strange and unfamiliar. You may have doubts and fears. That is okay. Be patient with yourself. Be gentle with yourself. This is a journey, not a destination. It is a relationship that will grow and deepen over time.

Do not be discouraged if you don't have a dramatic experience right away. Do not be discouraged if your mind wanders or if you feel like you are just talking to yourself. The saints are patient. They are not looking for a perfect performance. They are looking for an open heart. They seek a simple, honest desire to connect.

Start small. Start with the simple practices in this chapter. Choose a patron saint. Create a sacred space. Have a short, daily conversation. And then, see what happens. Pay attention. Be open. And trust that the God who has brought you this far will continue to lead you, step by step, into the beautiful, life-giving reality of the communion of saints.

You are not alone. You are part of a vast, loving, and powerful family. And they are so, so happy that you are finally coming home.

The Role of Imagination in Prayer

One of the most significant shifts in my own prayer life came when I began to understand the role of the imagination. In my Protestant upbringing, the imagination was often seen as a dangerous and deceptive faculty, a source of fantasy and illusion that could lead us away from the solid, objective truth of Scripture. Prayer was a matter of words, of thoughts, of the rational mind. It was not a matter of images, feelings, or sensory experiences.

However, the Celtic Christians, like many of the church's great contemplative traditions, held a more holistic view. They understood that God created us as whole beings—body, mind, and spirit—and that He wants to engage all of who we are in prayer. The imagination, for them, was not a distraction from prayer; it was a doorway into it. It was a God-given faculty that could help us to make the unseen world more real, more present, more tangible.

St. Ignatius of Loyola, the founder of the Jesuits, developed a powerful method of prayer based on this principle. He called it "composition of place." Before praying with a passage of Scripture, he would encourage his students to use their imagination to create the scene in their minds. To see the colours, to hear the sounds, to smell the smells. To place themselves in the story. This was not an exercise in fantasy; it was an act of faith. It was a way of saying, "I believe that this story is real, and I want to enter into it with my whole self."

We can use this same practice in our prayer with the saints. When you sit down to pray with St. Columba, don't just think about him as a historical figure. Use your imagination to place yourself with him. See him in your mind's eye. Is he on the windswept shores of Iona, his cloak flapping in the wind? Is he in the scriptorium, his head bent over a beautifully illuminated manuscript? Is he in the chapel, his face illuminated by the soft glow of candlelight? What does he look like? What is he wearing? What is the expression on his face?

This is not about creating a historically accurate portrait. We have no idea what St. Columba actually looked like. It is about using our imagination to make his presence more real to us. It is about moving from an abstract concept to a personal encounter. When you can see him in your mind's eye, it becomes much more natural to speak to him, to share your heart with him, to listen for his wisdom.

I do this all the time. When I am struggling with a difficult decision, I will often close my eyes and imagine myself walking with St. Patrick on the hills of Ireland. I see the green grass, I feel the soft mist on my face, I hear the bleating of the sheep. And I walk with him, and I tell him my troubles. And as I walk, I watch him. I see the quiet strength in his eyes, the gentle compassion in his smile. In that imagined encounter, I often find the clarity and courage I need.

This is not a form of new-age visualisation. It is a deeply Christian practice, rooted in the belief that the saints are truly present to us in the body of Christ. The imagination is simply the faculty that God has given us to perceive that presence more vividly. It is a bridge between the seen and the unseen, a way of making the thin place even thinner.

So, do not be afraid to use your imagination in prayer. It is not a distraction; it is a gift. It is a way of loving God and His saints with all of your mind, all of your heart, and all of your soul. It is a way of entering more fully into the beautiful, mysterious, and life-giving reality of the communion of saints.

Chapter 5:

Fasting and Prayer: Intensifying Your Spiritual Practice

For years, I avoided fasting. I admired it from a distance; in the same way, I admired people who run ultramarathons or climb Mount Everest. It was a practice for the spiritual elite, the superheroes of the faith, the men and women who were so far advanced on their journey that they could engage in these extreme forms of asceticism. It was not for me. I was a man who enjoyed his food, a man who found comfort in a good meal at the end of a long day. The idea of voluntarily giving that up felt not just tricky, but masochistic. It felt like a form of self-punishment, a way of telling God how serious you were by making yourself miserable.

And I had been miserable enough in my life. I wasn't looking for more of it.

My prayer life was active. My conversations with the saints were becoming more natural, more life-giving. I was reading the Scriptures, going to church, and trying to be a good husband and father. Wasn't that enough? Fasting felt like an unnecessary extra, a spiritual overachievement that had little to do with the messy, grace-filled reality of my daily life.

And so, I kept it at arm's length. I respected it, but I didn't practice it until the day my friend relapsed.

His name was Michael. He was one of the first men I had sponsored in a 12-step program, a young man whose story was hauntingly similar to my own. He had come from a background of violence and addiction, and he had found a fragile, beautiful sobriety. I had walked with him, prayed with him, shared my own story with him. I loved him like a brother. And then, one day, he was gone. He stopped answering his phone. He missed his meetings. And we all knew what that meant. He was back out there, in the darkness, in the chaos, in the life that was going to kill him.

I was frantic. I prayed. I called his family. I drove around to his old haunts, looking for him. Nothing. A week passed, and the silence was profound. I was filled with a sense of utter helplessness. I had done everything I knew how to do, and it wasn't enough. I was on my knees in my study, pleading with God to bring him back, and I felt like my prayers were hitting the ceiling.

In my desperation, I remembered something I had read about the early Celtic monks. When they were faced with a desperate situation, a spiritual battle that they could not win on their own, they would engage in a practice called the "black fast." It was a rigorous, multi-day fast of only bread and water, a way of laying siege to heaven, of saying to God, "We will not eat, we will not rest, until you have mercy on us."

It was a crazy idea. It was extreme. It was everything I had been avoiding. But I was desperate. And so, I decided to try it.

I told my wife what I was doing, and I began. The first day was miserable. My body screamed for food, for caffeine, for sugar. I was irritable, weak, and distracted. My prayers felt even more feeble than before. I was convinced this was a terrible mistake. But I kept going. I drank water. I ate a piece of dry bread. And I prayed. "Lord, have mercy on Michael. St. Columba, you know what it is to fight for a soul. Join me in this fight. We will not give up."

Something shifted on the second day. The physical hunger was still there, but it was no longer the loudest voice in the room. A quiet space had opened up inside me. My prayers were no longer a frantic, desperate monologue.

They were a quiet, steady, focused plea. I felt a profound sense of solidarity with Michael in his suffering. My own physical discomfort was a small, tangible way of entering into his pain, of sharing his burden.

On the third day, I felt a strange sense of lightness, of clarity. The world seemed sharper, brighter. The veil between heaven and earth felt incredibly thin. My prayers were no longer just words; they were a deep, silent communion. I felt the presence of the saints surrounding me, their prayers mingling with mine. I felt a profound sense of peace, a surrender to the will of God. I had done all I could do. The rest was up to Him.

That evening, my phone rang. It was Michael. He was crying. He was at a detox centre. He had hit rock bottom, and he had finally reached out for help. He was alive. He was safe. He was coming home.

I fell to my knees and wept, not with the frantic tears of desperation, but with the quiet, overwhelming tears of gratitude. I broke my fast that night with a simple bowl of soup, and it was the most delicious meal I have ever eaten. It was a meal of grace, a meal of resurrection, a meal that tasted of mercy.

That was the day I stopped being afraid of fasting. That was the day I learned that fasting is not a form of self-punishment, but a powerful weapon of spiritual warfare. It is not a way of making ourselves miserable to get God's attention, but a way of emptying ourselves so that we can be filled with His presence and His power.

It is the spiritual equivalent of turning up the volume on our prayers, of saying to God, to the saints, and to the powers of darkness, "We are serious about this. We will not be moved. We will not give up." In this chapter, we will explore this ancient and powerful practice. We will learn what it is, why it matters, and how we can incorporate it into our own journey of spiritual companionship.

What is Christian Fasting?

Before we can practice fasting, we must understand what it is. In our culture, fasting is most often associated with dieting or with political protest. It is a way to lose weight or to make a statement. But Christian fasting is something entirely different. It is not primarily about the body, nor is it about making a political point. It is a spiritual discipline, an act of worship, a form of prayer.

At its most basic, fasting is the voluntary abstention from food for a spiritual purpose. It is the act of saying "no" to a legitimate, God-given physical appetite to say a more profound "yes" to God. It is the recognition that we are not just physical beings, but spiritual beings, and that our spiritual hunger is more important than our physical hunger. It is the lived-out prayer of Jesus in the wilderness: "Man shall not live by bread alone, but by every word that comes from the mouth of God" (Matthew 4:4).

Christian fasting is not a hunger strike against God. It is not a way of twisting God's arm, of forcing Him to give us what we want. God is not a cosmic vending machine that dispenses blessings in exchange for our self-denial. Fasting does not change God; it changes us. It is a practice that re-orients our hearts, our minds, and our bodies toward God. It is a way of clearing out the clutter of our lives to make more space for Him.

Fasting is also not a way of earning God's favour. We cannot make ourselves more righteous or more holy through our own efforts. Our righteousness is a gift, received through faith in the finished work of Jesus Christ. Fasting is not a way of adding to that work; it is a way of responding to it. It is an act of gratitude, an expression of our love for the One who gave everything for us. It is a way of saying, "You are more important to me than food. You are more important to me than comfort. You are my all in all."

Finally, Christian fasting is not a solitary practice. It is something we do in communion with the whole church, both on earth and in heaven. When we fast, we are joining our small act of self-denial to the great, cosmic fast of the body of Christ throughout the ages. We are standing in solidarity with Moses on the mountain, with Esther before the king, with Jesus in the wilderness, with the early church in the book of Acts, with the desert fathers and mothers, with the Celtic saints. We are adding our voice to a great chorus of prayer and self-denial that has been rising to the throne of God for millennia. This is why fasting is such a powerful way to deepen our connection with the saints. When we fast, we are entering into their story. We are practising their discipline. We are joining their fight.

Biblical and Historical Foundations

Fasting is not a new or uniquely Christian practice. It has been a part of almost every major world religion for centuries. But it has a particular and profound meaning in the Judeo-Christian tradition. The story of the Bible is filled with men and women who fasted in times of crisis, repentance, discernment, and deep communion with God.

In the Old Testament, fasting was a common response to personal and national crisis. When the nation of Israel was threatened by its enemies, King Jehoshaphat "proclaimed a fast throughout all Judah" (2 Chronicles 20:3). When the prophet Jonah warned the city of Nineveh of God's impending judgment, the king and all the people "proclaimed a fast and put on sackcloth, from the greatest of them to the least of them" (Jonah 3:5).

Fasting was a way of humbling oneself before God, of acknowledging one's sin and dependence, and of crying out for mercy.

Fasting was also a way of preparing for a significant encounter with God or an important act of service.

Moses fasted for forty days and forty nights on Mount Sinai before receiving the Ten Commandments (Exodus 34:28).

Daniel fasted for twenty-one days while seeking a vision from God (Daniel 10:2-3).

Fasting was a means of clearing the spiritual channels, heightening one's spiritual sensitivity, and preparing oneself to receive a word from the Lord.

In the New Testament, Jesus Himself sets the example for us. He begins His public ministry with a forty-day fast in the wilderness (Matthew 4:1-11). This was a time of intense spiritual battle and of deep communion with His Father. It was the preparation for His entire life's work. And He assumed that His followers would fast as well. In the Sermon on the Mount, He gives instructions on how to fast: not with a gloomy face, to be seen by others, but in secret, as an act of worship known only to our Father in heaven (Matthew 6:16-18). He doesn't say "if you fast," but "when you fast." For Jesus, fasting was a normal and expected part of the spiritual life.

The early church continued this practice. In the book of Acts, we see the leaders of the church fasting and praying before making important decisions, such as sending out Paul and Barnabas on their first missionary journey (Acts 13:2-3). Fasting was a way of seeking God's guidance, of discerning His will, of consecrating their work to Him.

This practice was continued by the early church fathers and the desert monks, who regarded fasting as an essential means of taming the passions and cultivating a life of prayer. It was a practice embraced with particular zeal by the Celtic Christians. The lives of the Celtic saints are filled with stories of heroic fasting. St. Patrick is said to have fasted for forty days on the mountain that now bears his name, Croagh Patrick, wrestling with God for the salvation of Ireland. The monastic rules of saints like Columba and Columbanus prescribed regular and rigorous fasting as a core part of the ascetic life. For them, fasting was not an optional extra; it was the training ground of the soul. It was the gymnasium where the spiritual athlete was made strong.

So, when we fast today, we are not doing something strange or new. We are stepping into a deep and ancient stream of practice. We are walking in the footsteps of Moses and David, of Jesus and Paul, of Patrick and Columba. We are recovering a lost art, a powerful weapon, a beautiful act of worship that has been at the heart of our faith from the very beginning.

Why We Fast: The Fourfold Purpose

Why should we fast? What does it actually do? I have found it helpful to think of the purpose of fasting in four categories: Stillness, Solidarity, Strength, and Surrender.

1. To Create Space (Stillness): Our lives are incredibly noisy. We are constantly bombarded by information, by entertainment, by the demands of work and family. Our souls are cluttered and distracted. Fasting is a way of creating a quiet space amid this noise. When we voluntarily say "no" to something that usually fills our time and our attention—whether it is food, or social media, or entertainment—we create a vacuum. We create a space. And in that empty space, we can begin to hear the still, small voice of God. The physical hunger we feel becomes a reminder, a bell that calls us back to our spiritual hunger. The time we would have spent eating or scrolling becomes time for prayer, for reading, for silence. Fasting is a way of decluttering the soul, sweeping out the noise and distraction, and creating a quiet, uncluttered space where we can be present to God.

2. To Express Seriousness (Solidarity): There are times in our lives when our prayers have a particular urgency. We are praying for the healing of a loved one, for the salvation of a child, for guidance in a major life decision. Fasting is a way of expressing the seriousness of our prayer. It is a way of saying to God, to ourselves, and to the spiritual world, "This matters. This is not a casual request. I am all in." My desperate fast for my friend Michael was an expression of this kind of seriousness. I was saying, "I will not be distracted. I will not be deterred. I will pour all of my energy, all of my attention, all of my being into this prayer." Fasting is a way of aligning our bodies with our prayers. It is a way of praying with our whole selves. It is a way of standing in solidarity with those for whom we pray. When we fast for the hungry, our own hunger connects us to their suffering. When we fast for the sick, our own weakness connects us to their pain. It is a powerful act of empathy and love.

3. To Cultivate Discipline (Strength): We are creatures of appetite. We are driven by our desires for food, for comfort, for pleasure, for approval. And very often, these desires are in control. We are their slaves, not their masters. Fasting is a way of reclaiming our freedom. It is a way of training our will, of strengthening our spiritual muscles. Every time we feel a pang of hunger and choose to say "no" to it for the sake of our prayer, we are strengthening our ability to say "no" to other, more destructive desires. We are learning to be the masters of our own house. As I shared in the last chapter, this was a crucial part of my own journey. I was a man of immense passion but little discipline. Fasting, in communion with the saints who had mastered this art, was the gymnasium where I learned to order my passions, to channel my desires, and to become a man of spiritual strength and stability.

4. To Deepen Dependence (Surrender): In our modern, affluent world, it is easy to live under the illusion of self-sufficiency. We have food in our refrigerators, money in our bank accounts, and a thousand distractions at our fingertips. We can easily forget how utterly dependent we are on God for our very next breath. Fasting is a powerful antidote to this illusion. It is a voluntary embrace of weakness, of emptiness, of need. It is a way of reminding ourselves, in a visceral, embodied way, that we are not in control. We are creatures, utterly dependent on our Creator for everything. The physical hunger we feel becomes a spiritual teacher, instructing us in the fundamental truth of our existence: we live and move and have our being in God. Fasting is an act of surrender, a way of letting go of our pride and our self-sufficiency, and of casting ourselves completely on the mercy and the grace of God. It is the prayer of the poor in spirit, the prayer of the hungry, the prayer of the humble. And as Jesus reminds us, it is these who are blessed.

How to Fast: A Practical Guide

So, how do we do it? How do we move from understanding the "why" of fasting to practising the "how"? Here is a practical guide to getting started.

Types of Fasts: There are many different ways to fast. The key is to choose a fast that is appropriate for your health, your circumstances, and your spiritual goals.

• **Full Fast:** This is the most traditional form of fasting, where you abstain from all food and drink, except for water. This is a very intense form of fasting and should not be undertaken for more than a day or two without medical supervision.

• **Liquid Fast:** On a liquid fast, you abstain from all solid food but allow yourself to drink water, juice, or broth. This is a good way to undertake a longer fast (three to seven days) while still providing your body with some nourishment.

• **Partial Fast (or Daniel Fast):** This involves abstaining from certain types of food, such as meat, dairy, sugar, or processed foods. The "Daniel Fast," based on the story of Daniel in the Old Testament, is a popular form of partial fast that involves eating only fruits, vegetables, and whole grains. This is a great way to begin fasting, as it is less physically demanding yet still requires significant discipline.

• **Non-Food Fasts:** Fasting is not just about food. We can also fast from other things that hold our hearts and our time. You might consider a fast from social media, television, news, complaining, and gossip. The principle is the same: you are voluntarily giving up something that you usually consume to create more space for God.

The Rhythm of Fasting: Fasting is not meant to be a one-time, heroic effort. It is intended as a regular, rhythmic practice woven into the fabric of our lives.

• **Daily Fasting:** This might involve a form of intermittent fasting, such as eating only during an eight-hour window each day. Or it might be a fast from a particular thing for a day, such as a fast from complaining.

• **Weekly Fasting:** The early church had a practice of fasting every Wednesday and Friday. You might choose to adopt a weekly fast, such as a 24-hour liquid fast from after dinner on Thursday to after dinner on Friday. This is a powerful way to keep your spiritual life centred throughout the week.

• **Seasonal Fasting:** The church calendar provides us with seasons of fasting, such as Lent and Advent. These are times when the whole church is called to a period of intensified prayer, fasting, and almsgiving. Participating in these seasonal fasts is a beautiful way to connect with the wider body of Christ.

• **Intensive Fasting:** These are the fasts that we undertake for a specific, urgent purpose, like my fast for my friend Michael. These are not part of our regular rhythm, but are a response to a particular leading of the Holy Spirit.

The Three Stages of a Fast: A successful fast has three parts: preparation, the fast itself, and breaking the fast.

• **Preparation:** Before you begin a fast, especially a longer one, it is important to prepare both physically and spiritually. Physically, you might want to eat smaller, lighter meals for a day or two beforehand. Spiritually, you should be clear about your intention. Why are you fasting? What are you praying for? Write it down. Share it with your anam cara. Prepare your heart to meet with God.

• **During the Fast:** The time that you would typically spend eating should be filled with prayer, with reading the Scriptures, with silence. Rest is also important, particularly during longer fasts. Your body is under stress, so be gentle with it. And drink plenty of water!

• **Breaking the Fast:** How you break a fast is as important as the fast itself. Do not break a longer fast with a huge, heavy meal. Your digestive system has been resting, and you need to reintroduce food gradually. Begin with something light, such as soup or fruit. And break your fast with a prayer of gratitude.

Thank God for the grace He has given you, for the ways He has met you in your hunger.

Fasting with the Saints

Fasting is a powerful practice in itself. But it becomes even more powerful when we do it in communion with the saints. Fasting is a way of entering into their story, of practising their discipline, of joining our small sacrifice to their great cloud of witnesses.

How can we fast with the saints? Here are a few practical ways:

• **Ask for Their Companionship:** Before you begin a fast, ask your patron saint to be your companion. Ask them to pray for you, to support you, to teach you what they have learned about this practice. While learning the discipline of fasting, I asked St. Columbanus, the great, austere Irish monk, to be my guide. I knew he would not let me off the hook easily! His stern, loving companionship was exactly what I needed.

• **Fast for a Specific Intention with a Specific Saint:** If you are praying for a particular need, dedicate your fast to that intention and ask a saint with a connection to that need to join you. If you are fasting for the courage to share your faith, fast with St. Patrick. If you are fasting for a deeper connection to nature, fast with St. Kevin. This practice of dedicating a fast to a specific intention, in communion with a specific saint, can bring a powerful focus and clarity to your prayer.

• **Fast on a Saint's Feast Day:** The church calendar is filled with the feast days of the saints. Choosing to fast on the feast day of your patron saint, or another saint you are getting to know, is a beautiful way to honour them and to enter into the spirit of their life and witness. It is a way of saying, "On this day, when the whole church remembers you, I want to join my small act of self-denial to your great legacy of faith."

My own journey with fasting has been inextricably linked to my journey with the saints. They have been my teachers, my companions, my drill sergeants, and my cheerleaders. They have taught me that fasting is not about my own heroic effort, but about my humble participation in the great, cosmic struggle between light and darkness. And they have shown me that in my weakness, His strength is made perfect.

Practices for This Chapter

1. A Simple 24-Hour Fast: Choose one day this week and commit to a 24-hour fast. You might choose a liquid fast (water, juice, broth) or a complete fast (water only). Prepare for it, dedicate it to a specific intention, and fill the time you would normally spend eating with prayer. Break it gently, with a prayer of gratitude.

2. A Weekly Media Fast: Choose one day a week (or even just a few hours) to fast from all forms of media—social media, news, television, and podcasts. Use that time for silence, for reading, for prayer, for being present to the people around you. Notice the effect this has on your soul.

3. Fast with Your Patron Saint: On the feast day of your patron saint (you can find it online), or on another day you choose, dedicate a fast to them. It might be a fast from a particular food they were known to abstain from, or a fast from a particular sin they struggled with. Ask them to be your companion in the fast, and to pray for you that you might grow in the virtue that they so beautifully embodied.

The Eucharist: The Ultimate Fast and Feast

No discussion of Christian fasting is complete without the Eucharist. This may seem counterintuitive. The Eucharist, after all, is a meal. It is a feast. How can it be related to fasting? But in the deep logic of the Christian faith, the fast and the feast are two sides of the same coin. They are the rhythm of the Christian life, the dying and the rising, the emptying and the filling.

The Eucharist is the ultimate feast because it is the meal in which we are fed not with earthly food but with the very life of God. It is the meal where we receive the body and blood of Christ, the bread of heaven, the cup of salvation. It is the foretaste of the great wedding feast of the Lamb, the ultimate fulfilment of all our hunger and all our longing.

But the Eucharist is also the ultimate fast. It is the meal that re-orients all our other hungers. It is the meal that teaches us that we are made for more than bread alone. It is the meal that exposes the inadequacy of all the other things we feast on—the junk food of entertainment, the empty calories of consumerism, the sugar high of worldly success.

The Eucharist is the true food, and in its light, all other foods are revealed as what they are: temporary, partial, and ultimately unsatisfying.

This is why the ancient church consistently linked fasting to the Eucharist. The fast was the preparation for the feast. Christians would fast before receiving the Eucharist as a way of preparing their hearts, stirring up their spiritual hunger, and making space for the true food to come. The physical emptiness they felt was a tangible expression of their spiritual longing for Christ. And when they finally received the Eucharist, it was not just a routine ritual, but a joyful, grateful, and deeply satisfying feast.

This is a practice that we can apply in our own lives. We can fast before we come to the Lord's Table. It doesn't have to be a long or arduous fast. The Catholic Church has a tradition of a simple one-hour fast before Mass. But even this small act of self-denial can have a profound effect on our experience of the Eucharist. It is a way of saying, "Lord, I am hungry for you. I am empty without you. Fill me with your life."

And when we feast at the Lord's Table, we are not feasting alone. We are feasting with the entire communion of saints. The Eucharist is the church's family meal, and the whole family is invited. The saints in heaven are gathered with us around the same table, singing the same song of praise, feasting on the same Lamb of God. The Eucharist is the place where the veil between heaven and earth is at its thinnest. It is the place where, for a few sacred moments, we experience the reality of the one, undivided body of Christ.

My own journey with fasting has led me to a much deeper appreciation of the Eucharist. I used to see it as a nice symbol, a pleasant ritual. I now regard it as the very centre of my spiritual life. It is the place where my fasting finds its meaning and its fulfilment. It is the place where His grace meets my hunger. And it is the place where I am most deeply united with my heavenly family, the great cloud of witnesses, the communion of saints. It is the place where we, together, feast on the love of God.

A Final Word of Caution: Fasting and the Body

I want to end this chapter with a word of caution. In our enthusiasm for the spiritual benefits of fasting, we must be careful not to fall into a Gnostic or dualistic mindset that sees the body as evil or as a prison for the soul. This is not the Christian view. The Christian view is that the body is good. God created it, and Christ took it up in the Incarnation. Our bodies are not obstacles to our spiritual lives; they are the very means by which we live them. They are, as St. Paul says, "temples of the Holy Spirit" (1 Corinthians 6:19).

Therefore, our fasting must always be undertaken with a deep respect and love for our bodies. It is not about punishing the body, but about training it. It is not about hating the body, but about integrating it into our spiritual lives. It is about teaching our bodies to hunger for God.

This implies that we must be prudent in our fasting. We must listen to our bodies. We must not fast in a way that harms our health. If you have a medical condition, such as diabetes, or if you have a history of eating disorders, you should consult with a doctor and a spiritual director before undertaking a food-based fast. There are many other ways to fast—from media, from complaining, from comfort—that can be just as spiritually fruitful.

The goal of fasting is not to become a disembodied spirit. The goal of fasting is to become a more fully integrated human being, a person whose body, mind, and spirit are all oriented toward the love of God. The goal of fasting is to learn to live in our bodies in a new way, a way that is free from the tyranny of appetite and open to the leading of the Spirit. The goal of fasting is to make our whole lives, in our bodies, a living sacrifice, holy and acceptable to God.

This is the beautiful and challenging path that the saints have walked before us. They were not Gnostics who hated their bodies. They were lovers of God who loved their bodies enough to train them, to discipline them, to offer them back to God as a living prayer. And in doing so, they discovered a freedom and a joy that the world cannot give.

May we, by the grace of God and the companionship of the saints, learn to walk this path as well.

Chapter 6:

Meditation and Contemplation: Encountering the Saints

I had learned to talk to the saints. My prayer life, once a stilted and self-conscious performance, had become a real conversation. I spoke with Columba about my anger, with Patrick about my mission, with Brigid about my family. It was honest, raw, and life-changing. But it was also very noisy. My prayers were filled with my words, my thoughts, my needs, my struggles. I was doing all the talking. And I had a growing, gnawing suspicion that I was missing the most important part of the conversation.

I was a man who was comfortable with noise. My life before Christ had been filled with the noise of violence, of arguments, of the loud, desperate clamour of a soul at war with itself. My life in Christ was filled with the noise of ministry, of preaching, of writing, of raising a family. I was good at doing, at speaking, at acting. I was terrible at being still. The very idea of silence terrified me. When I tried to be silent, my mind would erupt in a cacophony of noise—a to-do list, a rehashed argument, a worry about the future, a song I had heard on the radio. It was what the Buddhists call "monkey mind," and my monkeys were on methamphetamines.

I confessed this to my anam cara, David. "I can't do it," I said, pacing his study. "I can't be silent. I try to listen, and all I hear is the chaos inside my own head. It's a complete failure. I'm just not built for this contemplative stuff."

David listened, as he always did, with a deep and patient quietness. When I had finally run out of steam, he smiled gently. "You're trying too hard, Stuart," he said. "You're trying to fight your thoughts, to wrestle them into submission. You're treating silence as an achievement, as something you have to accomplish. But silence is not an absence of noise. It is a presence. It is the presence of God. You don't have to create it. You have to consent to it."

He gave me a simple instruction, one that would change the course of my spiritual life. "Go to your sacred space," he said. "Sit down. Close your eyes. And just be. Don't try to empty your mind. That's impossible. Just notice your thoughts as they come and go, like clouds in the sky. Don't cling to them. Don't fight them. Just let them pass. And when you notice a thought has carried you away—and you will, a thousand times—just gently, without judgment, return to the present moment. Return to the presence of God who is right there with you, in the midst of the chaos."

It sounded too simple, too easy. But I was desperate enough to try. I went to my study. I lit my candle. I sat in my chair. And I tried to "just be." My mind, of course, went crazy. I thought about my sermon for Sunday, about the leaky faucet in the bathroom, about a hurtful comment someone had made. But each time I noticed I was lost in thought, I remembered David's words. "Gently, without judgment, return." And so, I did. Again and again and again.

I didn't "hear" anything. There were no visions, no angelic choirs. But after about twenty minutes of this gentle returning, something began to shift. The frantic energy in my soul began to quiet down. The monkeys were still there, but they seemed to have had a cup of chamomile tea. And in the space between my thoughts, I began to feel something. A quiet, steady, loving presence. It was the silence I had been so afraid of, but it was not an empty silence. It was complete silence. It was a silence that was alive, holding me, loving me.

And in that silence, a name surfaced in my heart: Kevin. St. Kevin of Glendalough, the hermit who was said to have stood so still in prayer that a blackbird built a nest in his outstretched hand. I had always been baffled by Kevin. His radical stillness seemed alien to my restless nature. But in that moment, I felt a strange kinship with him. I felt his companionship. He wasn't telling me to be like him.

He was being with me, in my own fumbling, imperfect attempt at stillness.

He was the quiet friend who knew the language of silence, and he was gently, patiently teaching it to me.

That was my first real experience of contemplative prayer. It was the day I learned that prayer is not just about speaking; it is about listening. It is not just about doing; it is about being. And it is in that quiet, receptive, listening space that we can begin to encounter the saints, not just as historical figures to be talked to, but as living companions to be with. In this chapter, we will explore this quiet and beautiful path. We will learn how to move from the noisy world of our own thoughts into the complete silence of God's presence, where the whispers of our heavenly friends can finally be heard.

From Speaking to Listening: The Two Lungs of Prayer

Prayer has often been described as the two lungs of the spiritual life: the active and the receptive. The active lung is the prayer of speaking, of doing. It is our petitions, our intercessions, our praise, our confession. It is the prayer we explored in the last chapter. It is essential. It is powerful. But it is only half of the equation.

The receptive lung is the prayer of listening, of being. It is the prayer of silence, of stillness, of waiting. It is the prayer where we stop talking and start listening. It is the prayer where we move from thinking about God to resting in God. This is the world of meditation and contemplation. For many, especially in the Protestant tradition, this receptive lung is underdeveloped.

We are masters of the active prayer. We know how to study the Bible, how to formulate our requests, and how to lead a prayer meeting. But we are often novices in the art of silence. The idea of simply being with God, without words, without an agenda, can feel unproductive, even lazy. But the great saints and mystics of the church have always taught that this receptive, contemplative prayer is the highest form of prayer. It is the prayer of lovers, who can sit together in comfortable silence, content to be in each other's presence. It is important to distinguish Christian meditation from the forms of meditation that have become popular in our culture, often drawn from Eastern religions. The goal of many Eastern meditation practices is emptiness, the cessation of thought, the dissolution of the self into a formless void. The goal of Christian meditation is the exact opposite. It is not emptiness, but fullness.

It is not the dissolution of the self, but the encounter with the ultimate Self, the great "I AM." It is union with a person, the person of Jesus Christ, in the communion of the Holy Spirit.

Christian meditation is not about emptying the mind, but about filling it with the things of God. It is the active, prayerful engagement of the mind with a sacred text, a sacred image, or a sacred truth. The early monks had a wonderful phrase for this: *ruminatio,* or "chewing." To meditate is to take a small piece of spiritual food—a verse of Scripture, a line from a saint's life—and to chew on it slowly, to turn it over and over in your mind, to savour its flavour, to allow its nutrients to be absorbed into your soul.

Contemplation is the next step. It is the fruit of meditation. Contemplation is a gift of grace. It is not something we can achieve through our own efforts. It is something we receive. It is the moment when the chewing stops, and we are left with the taste. It is the moment when we move from thinking about God to resting in God. It is a simple, loving gaze, a silent, wordless communion. It is the prayer of the heart, not the head. St. Teresa of Ávila, one of the greatest teachers of contemplative prayer, described it simply as "a close sharing between friends; it means taking time frequently to be alone with Him who we know loves us." This is the journey we are on in this chapter. We are learning to move from the active work of meditation to the quiet receptivity of contemplation. We are learning to cultivate inner silence in which we can not only speak to the saints but also hear their gentle whispers, feel their quiet companionship, and receive the wisdom they have to share.

Three Pathways into Contemplative Encounter

How do we begin this journey? How do we cultivate this inner silence? The Christian tradition has given us many beautiful and time-tested pathways. In this chapter, we will explore three of the most accessible and powerful: Lectio Divina (Sacred Reading), Visio Divina (Sacred Seeing), and Centring Prayer (The Prayer of the Heart).

1. Lectio Divina (Sacred Reading): Lectio Divina is an ancient practice of praying the Scriptures. It is a way of reading the Bible, not for information, but for formation. It is a way of listening for the voice of God speaking to us personally through the sacred text. It is a practice we can readily adopt to pray with the lives of the saints.
The practice has four simple steps:

• **Lectio (Read):** Choose a short passage of Scripture, or a short story from the life of a saint. Read it slowly, out loud if possible. Don't analyse it. Just received it. Listen to it with the ear of your heart.

- **Meditatio (Meditate):** Reread the passage. This time, listen for a word or phrase that stands out to you. Take that word or phrase and begin to "chew" on it. Repeat it to yourself. Savour it. Ask, "What is God saying to me in this word?"

- **Oratio (Pray):** Read the passage a third time. Now, respond to God. Your meditation will naturally flow into prayer. It might be a prayer of praise, of repentance, of gratitude, or of petition. Speak to God and to the saint about what has been stirred up in your heart.

- **Contemplatio (Contemplate):** Read the passage one last time. And then, rest. Let go of all your thoughts, all your words. Rest in the silent, loving presence of God and His saints. This is the practice's goal. It is the moment of quiet communion, of wordless love.

I remember the first time I did this with the life of a saint. I chose a story about St. Brigid. It was the story of how she gave away her father's entire store of butter to the poor. Her father was furious and was about to strike her when she prayed, and the butter was miraculously replenished. As I read the story, the word that shimmered for me was "give." I meditated on that word. I thought about my own struggles with generosity, my fear of not having enough. My prayer was a simple, "Brigid, you were so free, so generous. Pray for me, that I might have a heart like yours." And then I just rested in the presence of this woman of radical, joyful generosity. In that silence, I didn't hear a voice, but I felt a shift in my own heart, a loosening of my own tight-fisted grip on my possessions.

2. Visio Divina (Sacred Seeing): Visio Divina is the practice of praying with a sacred image, such as an icon. In the Eastern Orthodox tradition, icons are not just religious art; they are "windows into heaven." They are a place of encounter, a thin place where the veil between the seen and the unseen is drawn back. Praying with an icon is a powerful way to connect with a saint, to enter into their story, and to receive their blessing.

The practice is similar to Lectio Divina:

- **Gaze:** Sit quietly with the icon. Let your eyes rest on it. Don't analyse it. Just gaze at it with a soft, receptive focus.

- **Notice:** Begin to notice the details. The colours, the lines, the gestures, the expression on the saint's face. What do you see? What stands out to you?

- **Enter:** Allow yourself to enter into the scene. Imagine yourself in the presence of the saint. What do you want to say to them? What do they want to say to you? Listen with the ear of your heart.

- **Rest:** Let go of all your thoughts and observations. Rest in the saint's presence. Allow their peace, their strength, their love to wash over you. Receive their blessing.

As I shared in the previous chapter, my first genuine prayer to St. Columba was offered before a simple printed icon. That icon has become a dear friend. I have spent numerous hours examining it. I have noticed the intensity in his eyes, the passion that is not just anger, but a fierce love for God. I have noticed the book he holds, a symbol of his love for the Scriptures. I have noticed the small church in the background, a symbol of his mission to build communities of faith. And as I have gazed at this image, I have felt his presence, his companionship, his encouragement. That simple piece of paper has become a true window into heaven for me.

3. Centring Prayer (The Prayer of the Heart): Centring Prayer is a simple method of silent prayer that helps us to move from the active mind to the quiet heart. It is a way of consenting to God's presence and action within us. It is the practice that my friend David taught me, the practice that opened the door to my first real experience of contemplation.

The method is simple:

- **Choose a Sacred Word:** Choose a simple, one or two-syllable word that represents your intention to consent to God's presence. It might be "Jesus," "Love," "Peace," or "Abba." This is not a mantra to be repeated; it is a symbol of your intention.

- **Sit in Silence:** Sit comfortably, with your back straight. Close your eyes. And for a moment, be. Notice the sounds around you. Notice the sensations in your body. Notice your breath.

- **Introduce the Sacred Word:** Silently, gently, introduce your sacred word as a symbol of your consent to God's presence and action within.

- **Gently Return:** When you notice a thought has carried you away—and you will, a thousand times—gently, without judgment, return to your sacred word. The thoughts are not the enemy. The practice is not about having a blank mind. The practice is the gentle, patient, repeated act of returning.

That's it. You might set a timer for twenty minutes. At the end, remain in silence for a few moments, and then perhaps close with the Lord's Prayer. This practice is a training in letting go. It is a training in being present. It is a training in listening. And in the deep, interior silence this practice cultivates, we can begin to feel the subtle, non-verbal companionship of the saints. It was in this silence that I first felt the quiet, steady presence of St. Kevin. I didn't need to talk to him. I just needed to be with him. And in that shared stillness, I found a peace that I had never known.

The Fruits of Silence

This journey into silence, into the receptive lung of prayer, is not easy. It requires patience, perseverance, and considerable gentleness toward ourselves. But the fruits of this practice are profound. When we learn to be still and to listen, we begin to experience the communion of saints not as a theological concept but as a lived reality.

We begin to feel their presence with us, not only in our times of formal prayer but also in the midst of our daily lives. We begin to hear their gentle guidance, not as an audible voice, but as a quiet intuition, a sudden insight, a nudge in the right direction. We begin to draw strength from their example, courage from their witness, and peace from their prayers.

And perhaps most importantly, we begin to realise that we are part of a story that is much bigger than our own. We are part of a great cosmic family, a river of faith that has flowed for centuries. And the saints are our ancestors, our elders, our guides. They are the ones who have gone before us, who have marked the path for us, and who are now cheering us on from the heavenly stands. To learn to listen for their voices is to learn to listen for the heartbeat of the church, the heartbeat of Christ Himself. It is to come home.

Practices for This Chapter

1. Practice Lectio Divina: Choose a short story from the life of your patron saint. Spend at least twenty minutes this week practising the four steps of Lectio Divina with that story. Which word or phrase resonates with you? What is God saying to you through the life of this saint?

2. Practice Visio Divina: Find an icon or another sacred image of a saint that you are drawn to. Spend at least twenty minutes this week practising Visio Divina with that image. Gaze at it. Notice the details. Enter into the scene. And then, rest in the presence of the saint. What do you experience?

3. Practice Centring Prayer: Commit to practising Centring Prayer for twenty minutes every day for one week. Choose your sacred word. And then, practice the gentle, patient act of returning. Don't worry about whether you are "succeeding." Just do it. At the end of the week, notice if there has been any shift in your inner life, in your sense of peace, in your awareness of God's presence.

The Celtic Saints and the Contemplative Path

The Celtic saints were masters of this contemplative path. While they were also men and women of great action—missionaries, scholars, community builders—their action was always rooted in a deep well of contemplative stillness. They understood that fruitful ministry flows from a life of deep communion with God. Their lives were a beautiful dance between the active and the receptive, between doing and being, between speaking and listening.

We see this in the life of St. Patrick. He was a man of incredible energy and courage, a missionary who travelled the length and breadth of Ireland, confronting pagan kings and establishing churches. But his Confession reveals that a life of constant prayer fueled this tireless activity. He writes, "In a single day I have said as many as a hundred prayers, and in the night a like number." He speaks of rising before dawn to pray in the woods and on the mountains, in snow and in rain. His action was not a substitute for his prayer; it was the fruit of it.

We see this in the life of St. Columba. He was a great leader, the founder of the monastery on Iona, a spiritual father to countless monks. But he was also a poet and a scribe, a man who loved the quiet, patient work of copying the Scriptures. And he had a practice of retreating to a small, isolated cell on the edge of the island for periods of solitary prayer and contemplation. He knew that he could not lead others into the presence of God if he were not regularly entering into it himself.

And we see this, perhaps most profoundly, in the life of St. Kevin of Glendalough. Kevin was a true hermit, a man who fled from the world to seek God in the solitude of nature. His life was a radical witness to the power of stillness, of listening, of simply being present to God in creation. The story of the blackbird building a nest in his hand is a beautiful symbol of this. He was so lost in contemplative prayer, so at one with the world around him, that he became a safe place for a wild creature to make its home. This is the fruit of a deep contemplative life. We become people of peace, people who are so at home in ourselves and in God that we become a source of peace for others.

These saints are our guides on the contemplative path. They have walked this road before us. They know the challenges of a restless mind. They know the fear of silence. And they know the profound joy and peace that can be found on the other side. When we practice these contemplative disciplines, we are not just following a method; we are entering into their school of prayer. We are allowing them to teach us, to guide us, to accompany us into the deep, quiet heart of God. I have found this to be true in my own life. When I am struggling with the discipline of Centring Prayer and my mind is particularly chaotic, I often recall the image of St. Kevin. I will imagine him standing in the cold waters of the lake at Glendalough, his arms outstretched in prayer. I will feel his quiet, steady, patient presence with me. And I will ask him to pray for me, that I might have a portion of his stillness, his trust, his deep at-homeness in God. And in that moment, the struggle does not necessarily cease, but I am no longer alone in it. I am a fumbling student, sitting at the feet of a master, and I am content to learn, slowly and patiently, the beautiful and life-giving art of silence.

THE DARK NIGHT OF THE SOUL: WHEN THE SAINTS SEEM SILENT

No discussion of contemplative prayer would be complete without an honest acknowledgement of what the great mystic St. John of the Cross called "the dark night of the soul." There will be times in our spiritual journey when God and the saints seem utterly silent, utterly absent. Our prayers will feel like they are hitting a brass ceiling. Our times of meditation will feel dry, empty, and fruitless. The consolations and the sweet feelings of God's presence that we once enjoyed will be gone. And we will be left in a place of darkness, of confusion, of spiritual desolation.

This is a terrifying and painful experience. It can feel like we have done something wrong, like God has abandoned us, like our faith has been a sham. But the great saints and mystics teach us that this dark night is not a sign of

God's absence, but of His presence in a new and deeper way. It is a gift, a grace, a necessary stage in the journey of transformation.

In the early stages of our spiritual life, God often gives us many consolations. We feel His presence, we experience emotional highs in prayer, and we are filled with a sense of peace and joy. These are gifts, meant to draw us to Himself. But if we become attached to these gifts, if we begin to seek the consolations of God rather than the God of consolations, then our spiritual life can become a subtle form of self-gratification. We are in it for the good feelings.

The dark night is God's way of purifying our love. He withdraws the feelings of His presence so that we will learn to love Him for His own sake, not for the gifts He gives. He is weaning us off the milk of spiritual consolation and inviting us to eat the solid food of a mature faith, a faith that can trust in His goodness even when we cannot feel it. He is teaching us to walk by faith, not by sight.

This is a time when the companionship of the saints is especially important. They have all walked through this darkness. St. Teresa of Calcutta, for example, lived in a state of profound spiritual darkness for the last fifty years of her life. She felt no sense of God's presence, only a deep and painful longing for Him. And yet, she persevered in her life of prayer and service. She held fast to her faith, even in the absence of all feeling. And her witness has become a powerful source of hope and encouragement for all who walk this difficult path.

When you find yourself in the dark night, do not despair. You are in good company. Turn to the saints who have known this darkness. Read their stories. Pray with their words. Ask for their companionship. They will not necessarily eliminate the darkness. But they will walk with you in it. They will be a silent, steady presence, reminding you that you are not alone, that this darkness is not the end of the story, and that the dawn will come. They will teach you how to hope in the dark. And they will show you that it is often in the darkest nights that the stars shine most brightly.

I have had my own seasons of this darkness. Times when my prayers felt empty, when the saints seemed a million miles away, when God Himself felt like a cruel and distant abstraction. These have been the most painful and challenging times of my life. But they have also been the times of my deepest growth. It was in the darkness that I learned to let go of my own spiritual agendas, my own need for results, my own attachment to good feelings. It was in the darkness that I learned to trust, to surrender, to hope against hope. And it was in the darkness that I discovered a deeper, more resilient, and more compassionate faith.

If you are in such a season now, be gentle with yourself. Do not try to force a feeling that is not there. Be faithful to your practices of prayer and meditation, even if they feel empty. And lean on the companionship of your heavenly family. They know this road. They will see you through. And they will be there to celebrate with you when the morning comes.

THE GOAL OF CONTEMPLATION: UNION WITH GOD

What is the ultimate goal of this contemplative journey? It is not just about having enjoyable spiritual experiences or feeling a sense of peace. The goal is union with God. It is to arrive at a place where our will is so aligned with God's will, our heart so united with His heart, that we can say with St. Paul, "It is no longer I who live, but Christ who lives in me" (Galatians 2:20). This is the great promise of the Christian life. It is the destination to which all our practices of prayer, meditation, and contemplation are leading.

This union is not a loss of our own personality. It is the fulfilment of it. We do not become less ourselves; we become more ourselves, the person God created us to be from all eternity. C.S. Lewis used a beautiful analogy for this. He said that when we come to God, we are like a living stone that a master sculptor is shaping. The process can be painful. We feel the chisel and the hammer. But the sculptor is not trying to destroy us; He is trying to make us into a beautiful and unique work of art, a perfect reflection of His own glory.

This is what we see in the lives of the saints. They were not a collection of bland, generic holy people. They were vibrant, unique, and often eccentric personalities. St. Francis of Assisi was a poet and a lover of nature. St. Catherine of Siena was a fiery political activist. St. Thérèse of Lisieux was a quiet, hidden soul who found God in the small, ordinary duties of her life. Each of them was a unique expression of God's infinite creativity. And yet, in all of them, we see the face of Christ. They had been so transformed by their union with Him that His love, His joy, His peace, His compassion shone through them.

This invitation is also extended to us. We are invited to become saints, to become people who are so united with God that His life flows through us into the world. This is not a goal that we can achieve through our own efforts. It is a work of grace. But it is a work that requires our cooperation. It requires our "yes." It requires our commitment to the daily, patient, and often unspectacular work of prayer, meditation, and contemplation.

We do not have to undertake this work alone. The saints are not just our examples; they are our companions and our helpers on this journey. They are the ones who have already arrived at the destination, and they are reaching back to help us along the way. They are the master sculptors' apprentices, helping to shape us into the image of Christ. When we open ourselves to their companionship and invite them into our practice, we are availing ourselves of a powerful source of grace and assistance.

I have experienced this in my own life. There are times in my contemplative prayer when I feel stuck, like I am going in circles. In those moments, I often call upon a saint who was a master of the contemplative life, such as St. John of the Cross or St. Teresa of Ávila. I will ask them to pray for me, to guide me, to teach me. And I have often found that in the quiet space of that prayer, a new path opens, a new insight is given, and a new grace is received.

This is the great secret of the communion of saints. It is not just a beautiful doctrine; it is a practical reality. It is a network of love, of prayer, of mutual support that spans heaven and earth. And we are all invited to be a part of it. We are all invited to take our place in this great family, to receive the help of those who have gone before us, and to offer our own small prayers and sacrifices for the sake of those who will come after us.

So, as you embark on this contemplative journey, do not be afraid. You are not alone. A great cloud of witnesses surrounds you. You are held in the loving embrace of a family that is bigger and more beautiful than you can possibly imagine.

And you are being led, step by step, into the very heart of God.

Chapter 7:

Devotional Practices: Honouring the Saints in Daily Life

For a long time, my faith was a faith of the head. It lived in books, in sermons, in theological arguments. It was a faith of words and ideas. And I was proud of that. I had come out of a world of chaos and violence, and I had found a faith that was ordered, rational, and intellectually robust. I had a deep suspicion of anything that smacked of "smells and bells," of the physical, sensory, and emotional dimensions of faith. To me, that was the stuff of superstition, of empty ritual, of the "popish religion" I had been taught to distrust. My faith was pure. It was a matter of the mind and the will. It was clean, uncluttered, and safely contained between my ears.

And then I met David. As I've shared, David was my anam cara, the soul friend who guided me into the deeper waters of the Christian life. His faith was just as intellectually rigorous as mine, but it was also something more. It was earthy. It was embodied. It was beautiful. And his house was the first place I encountered this in a way that I couldn't ignore.

I remember the first time I went to his home for dinner. Tucked into a corner of his living room was a small, beautifully arranged table. On it was a simple wooden cross, a few icons, a candle, a well-worn Bible, and a small bowl of water. My internal heresy alarm went off. It looked like a shrine. It looked… Catholic. I remember thinking, "What is all this stuff? You don't need this to pray. It's just a bunch of religious clutter." I didn't say anything, of course, but I'm sure my judgment was written all over my face.

Later that evening, as we were talking, I finally got up the courage to ask him about it. "What's with the… corner?" I asked, trying to sound casual.

David smiled. He knew exactly what I was asking.

"That's my home altar," he said. "It's my sacred space. It's the place where I begin and end my day. It's the place where I meet with God."

"But you can meet with God anywhere," I countered, feeling the need to defend my more "spiritual" and less "religious" faith. "You don't need all that... stuff."

"You're right," he said, his voice gentle, not defensive. "I can meet with God anywhere. And I do. But I am a creature of body and soul, Stuart. I am not a disembodied spirit. God made me with five senses, and He wants to meet me through them. That little table is not a magic portal. The icons are not idols. They are reminders. They are doorways. They are physical, tangible things that help my scattered, distractible mind to focus on the unseen, spiritual reality of God's presence. They help me to remember who I am and whose I am."

His words hit me like a ton of bricks. I had been so proud of my "head-faith," but I was beginning to realise that it was a disembodied faith. It was a faith that was disconnected from my body, from my senses, from the physical world that God had created and called "good." I was living as if the Incarnation hadn't happened, as if God hadn't taken on flesh and blood, as if He hadn't entered into our messy, physical world to redeem it.

That conversation was the beginning of a new journey for me, a journey into the world of devotional practices. It was a journey of learning to pray with my whole self, my senses, my imagination, my heart. It was a journey of discovering that the physical world is not a distraction from the spiritual, but a sacrament of it.

And it was a journey of learning to honour the saints, not just as theological concepts but as real, present friends, by weaving their memory and companionship into the very fabric of my daily life. In this chapter, we will explore some of these ancient and beautiful practices. We will learn how to create our own sacred spaces, how to pray with icons, how to celebrate the feast days of the saints, and how to make our whole lives a pilgrimage of love.

The Principle of Sacramentality: God's Love in Physical Form

Before we dive into the specific practices, we need to understand the theological principle that underlies all of them: the principle of sacramentality. This is a beautiful and profoundly biblical idea that is at the heart of the Celtic Christian worldview. It is the belief that God uses physical, created things—water, bread, wine, oil, light, stone, wood—to communicate His unseen, spiritual grace. It is believed that the physical world is not a barrier to God but a bridge to Him.

This principle is rooted in the two great bookends of the Christian story: Creation and Incarnation. In the beginning, God created the physical world and called it "good" (Genesis 1). The world is not a mistake, not a prison for the soul. It is a gift, a masterpiece, a revelation of God's own beauty, goodness, and creativity. The heavens declare the glory of God, and the firmament shows His handiwork (Psalm 19:1).

The Celtic saints understood this deeply. They saw the face of Christ in the rising sun, they heard the voice of the Spirit in the cry of the wild goose, they felt the embrace of the Father in the strength of the ancient oak. For them, creation was a second book of revelation, a living, breathing sacrament of God's presence.

And then, in the fullness of time, the God who created the world entered into it. The Word became flesh and dwelt among us (John 1:14). This is the ultimate expression of sacramentality. God did not remain a distant, abstract spirit. He took on a body. He had hands and feet, a voice and a face. He ate and drank, He laughed and wept, He got tired, and He bled. In Jesus, God sanctified the physical. He showed us that our bodies are not something to be escaped, but something to be redeemed. He showed us that the path to the spiritual is not around the physical, but through it.

This is why the church has always used physical things in its worship. We are baptised with water, we are fed with bread and wine, we are anointed with oil. These are not just empty symbols. They are sacraments. They are physical, tangible means by which God communicates His grace to us. They are the extension of the Incarnation into the life of the church.

Devotional practices are a further extension of this sacramental principle into our daily lives. When we light a candle, when we gaze at an icon, when we make a pilgrimage to a holy place, we are not engaging in magic or superstition. We are engaging in embodied prayer. We are using the physical to connect with the spiritual. We are honouring the way that God made us, as integrated beings of body and soul. And we are pushing back against the Gnostic heresy that has haunted the church from the beginning, the heresy that says that the spirit is good and the body is bad. No. The body is good. The world is good. And God wants to meet us in the midst of it.

The Home Altar: Creating a Sacred Space

My journey into this embodied faith began with that conversation with David. I went home that night and looked around my house. It was a Christian home, to be sure. There were Bibles on the shelves, a cross on the wall. But there was no focal point. No place was set apart, no place that said, "This is where we meet with God."

And so, I decided to create one. It felt awkward and self-conscious. I didn't have a fancy table or beautiful icons. I cleared a small space on a bookshelf in my study. I found a simple, unadorned cross that my son had made in Sunday school. I printed out a small, black-and-white image of St. Columba from the internet and put it in a cheap frame. I found a smooth, grey stone from my garden and a small votive candle. It wasn't much, but it was a start. It was my first home altar.

And a funny thing happened. That little corner of my study began to change. It became a magnet for my spiritual life. In the morning, before the chaos of the day began, I would find myself drawn to it. I would light the candle, and in that small act, I would be reminded that I was entering into a sacred time, a sacred space. I would look at the cross and remember God's love. I would look at Columba's icon and remember that I was not alone in my struggles. I would hold the stone in my hand and feel a connection to the good, solid earth that God had made. My prayers, which had often been a scattered, distracted affair, began to have a focus, a centre, a home.

That simple, homemade altar became a thin place in my own house. It became the place where I wrestled with God, where I confessed my sins, where I offered my gratitude, where I felt the quiet companionship of the saints. It became the spiritual hearth of my home, the place to which I would return again and again to be warmed by the fire of God's love.

Creating a home altar is a simple and powerful way to begin to practice an embodied faith.

It is a way to carve out a physical space in your home dedicated to your relationship with God.

It is a way of saying, "In this house, we will serve the Lord."

What is a home altar? It is simply a small space in your home that you set apart for prayer and devotion. It is not a place of sacrifice, as the Old Testament altars were. It is a place of remembrance, a place of focus, a place of encounter.

Why have one? A home altar serves several purposes. It is a visual reminder of God's presence in your home. It is a focal point for your personal and family prayer. It is a way of honouring the liturgical seasons of the church year. And it is a way of creating a tangible connection to the communion of saints.

How do you create one? It can be as straightforward or as elaborate as you like. You can use a small table, a corner of a bookshelf, or a mantelpiece. The key is that it is a space set apart, not cluttered with the ordinary stuff of life. On your altar, you might place:

• **A Cross or Crucifix:** The central symbol of our faith, reminding us of the sacrificial love of Christ.

• **A Candle:** A symbol of Christ as the light of the world, and a way of marking your prayer time as sacred.

• **A Bible:** The living Word of God, the foundation of our faith.

• **Icons:** Images of Christ, Mary, and the saints, reminding us of our heavenly family.

• **Natural Objects:** A stone, a shell, a flower, a bowl of water—reminders of God's presence in creation.

• **Items that reflect the liturgical season:** Purple cloth for Lent, a wreath for Advent, flowers for Easter.

How do you use it?

Your home altar can become the centre of your devotional life. You can begin and end your day there with a short prayer. You can gather there with your family for evening prayers. You can light the candle when you are praying for a special intention. It is not a magic charm. It is a tool. It is a place. It is a home for your heart.

Icons: Windows into Heaven

As my home altar became a more central part of my life, I found myself drawn to the icons more and more. That cheap, black-and-white printout of St. Columba became a dear friend. I would gaze at it during my prayer time, and as I did, I began to see things I hadn't noticed before. I saw the passion in his eyes, a fire that was not just anger, but a fierce love for God. I saw the book he held, a symbol of his devotion to the Scriptures. I saw the small church in the background, a symbol of his mission to build communities of faith. That simple image became a window, a doorway into his story, into his spirit.

I began to read about the theology of icons.

I learned that in the Eastern Orthodox tradition, icons are not just religious art; they are a form of revelation. They are a theology in colour. They are written, not painted, according to a strict set of conventions that are designed to communicate theological truth, not just artistic expression.

I learned that icons are not meant to be a realistic, photographic representation of a person. They are intended to be a glimpse into their transfigured, glorified state in heaven. That is why the figures in icons often seem elongated, why the perspective is often "wrong," and why the light appears to emanate from within the figure rather than from an external source. The icon is not showing us what the saint looked like on earth; it is showing us what they look like now, in the light of God's glory.

And I learned the crucial distinction between worship and veneration. We do not worship icons. We do not worship the saints. We worship God alone. But we do venerate icons. We honour them. We show them respect. We kiss them, we bow before them, we light candles in front of them. Why? Because the honour we give to the image passes on to the one who is represented. When I kiss the icon of St. Columba, I am not kissing a piece of wood and paint. I am expressing my love and my gratitude to my brother and my friend in Christ. It is no different than kissing a photograph of my wife or my children when I am away from them. The photograph is not them, but it is a powerful reminder of them, a tangible connection to them.

This understanding freed me from my old fear of idolatry. I began to collect other icons—of Christ, of Mary, of Patrick, Brigid and Kevin. My home altar began to look more and more like a family photo album. And my prayer life was immeasurably enriched. The practice of Visio Divina, or "sacred seeing," which we explored in the last chapter, became a central part of my contemplative practice. I would spend time gazing at an icon, letting its beauty and its truth sink deep into my soul. And in that gazing, I would often feel a profound sense of connection, of communion, of being seen and loved by the one who was gazing back at me.

Icons are not essential for a relationship with the saints. But they are a powerful and beautiful aid. They are a gift from the ancient church, a way of engaging our senses in the act of prayer, a way of making the unseen world of the saints more visible, more tangible, more real.

Feast Days: Living in a Different Story

My journey into an embodied faith continued with a new understanding of time. For most of my life, my year was structured by the secular calendar: New Year's Day, the Fourth of July, Thanksgiving, and Christmas. It was a calendar of holidays and work schedules, of tax deadlines and school vacations. But as I delved deeper into the Celtic tradition, I discovered another calendar, another story, another rhythm for my life: the liturgical calendar.

This is the church's calendar, the one structured not around secular events but around the great story of our salvation. It begins in Advent, with the watchful waiting for the coming of Christ. It moves to Christmas, with the celebration of His birth. It journeys through Epiphany, Lent, Holy Week, and Easter, reliving the story of His life, death, and resurrection. And it continues through the long season of Pentecost, the season of the Spirit, the season of the church.

And woven into this great story are the feast days of the saints. These are the days that the church has set aside to remember and to celebrate the lives of the men and women who have gone before us in the faith. They are their heavenly birthdays, the days they entered into the fullness of God's glory. And to celebrate these days is to do more than remember a historical figure. It is to celebrate with them. It is to join our voices with the whole church, on earth and in heaven, in thanking God for their life and their witness.

I remember the first time I celebrated St. Patrick's Day as a feast day, rather than as an excuse to drink green beer.

I spent the morning reading his Confession.

I was moved to tears by his story of being kidnapped as a boy, of being a slave in a foreign land, and of hearing the call of God to return to the very people who had enslaved him to bring them the Gospel.

I spent some time in prayer, thanking God for Patrick's courage, faithfulness, and incredible love for the Irish people.

I asked him to pray for me, that I might have a portion of his missionary zeal. For dinner that night, my wife made a simple Irish stew. And as we ate, we told our children the story of St. Patrick. It was a simple celebration, yet profound.

I felt a deep connection to this spiritual giant, this apostle to the Irish. He was no longer just a character in a history book; he was a member of my family. And we were celebrating his birthday.

Celebrating the feast days of the saints is a powerful way to weave their stories into the fabric of our own. It is a way of living in a different story, a story that is bigger, richer, and more meaningful than the one our culture offers us. It is a way of populating our year with heroes, with mentors, with friends.

How can you begin to celebrate the feast days? Here are a few simple ideas:

• **Get a liturgical calendar:** Find out when the feast days of your patron saint and other saints you are drawn to are celebrated.

• **Read their story:** On their feast day, take some time to read a story from their life or a passage from their writings.

• **Pray with them:** Spend some time in prayer, thanking God for their witness and asking for their intercession.

• **Eat a special meal:** You might try to cook a meal from the country where the saint lived, or share a favourite meal with your family in their honour.

- **Do an act of service:** Do something that reflects the particular charism of the saint. On the feast of St. Francis, you might donate to an animal shelter. On the feast of St. Brigid, you might offer hospitality to a stranger.

- **Fast:** As we discussed in the last chapter, fasting is a powerful way to honour a saint and to enter into the spirit of their life of self-denial.

By celebrating the feast days, we begin to inhabit a new and more beautiful world. We begin to see that our lives are part of a great, ongoing story, a story filled with heroes and heroines, with drama and grace. And we begin to realise that we are not just a collection of individuals, but a family, a communion, a people who are bound together by a shared love for a common Lord.

Pilgrimage: The Journey of the Heart

The final devotional practice we will explore is pilgrimage. For the Celtic Christians, pilgrimage was one of the most important spiritual disciplines. It was a journey to a holy place, a thin place, a place hallowed by the presence of a saint. But it was more than just a physical journey. It was an outer journey that reflected an inner journey. It was a journey of the heart.

The great Celtic pilgrimage was the peregrinatio pro Christo, the "wandering for Christ." This was a radical act of faith: a monk would leave his home, his family, his monastery, and set out in a small, rudderless boat, trusting that the winds and waves of the Spirit would carry him to the place where God wanted him to be. It was an act of complete surrender, of letting go of all earthly security and casting oneself completely on the providence of God. It was from these radical acts of pilgrimage that many of the great Celtic monasteries were founded, on remote islands like Iona and Lindisfarne.

Most of us are not called to this kind of radical, life-altering pilgrimage. But we are all called to be pilgrims. We are all on a journey, a journey from this world to the next, a journey into the heart of God. And we can undertake our own, smaller pilgrimages to embrace this pilgrim identity.

I used to think that a pilgrimage had to be a grand, expensive trip to a famous holy site like Iona or Santiago de Compostela. And such pilgrimages can be powerful and life-changing. But I have come to believe that the spirit of pilgrimage is something that we can cultivate right where we are.

I remember the first time I went to my little oak grove in the park, intending to make a pilgrimage. I didn't just go for a walk. I went with a purpose. I went as a pilgrim. I left my phone in the car. I walked in silence, paying attention to the sights and the sounds around me.

I walked with a question in my heart, a question I was bringing to God and to my companion, St. Columba. And when I arrived at the grove, I didn't just sit on a bench. I sat on the ground. I felt the earth beneath me. I prayed. I listened. And I returned home with a sense of having been on a journey, of having been to a holy place, of having been met by God.

We can think of pilgrimage in three ways:

- **The Great Pilgrimage:** This is the journey to a major holy site. It requires time, planning, and resources. But it can be a powerful and transformative experience. To walk the same ground as the saints, to pray in the same places where they prayed, is to connect with them in a deep and embodied way.

- **The Local Pilgrimage:** This is a journey to a holy place in your own area. It might be a beautiful old church, a shrine, a monastery, a retreat centre, or a place of natural beauty. The key is to go with the intention of a pilgrim, with a prayer in your heart, with an openness to encountering God.

- **The Inner Pilgrimage:** This is the journey that we can take at any time, in any place. It is the journey of the heart into the presence of God. It is the journey we take when we sit in silence, when we practice contemplative prayer, when we turn our attention from the outer world to the inner landscape of our own souls. This is the most important pilgrimage of all, and it is the one to which all outer pilgrimages are meant to lead.

To be a pilgrim is to be a person who is on the way. It is to be someone who knows this world is not our final home. It is to be a person who travels light, who is not weighed down by the love of possessions or the fear of the unknown. And it is to be a person who knows that we do not travel alone. We travel in the company of the saints, our fellow pilgrims, who have gone before us and who are now cheering us on from our true and final home.

A Day in a Devotional Life

How does all of this come together? How do these practices look in the midst of a busy, ordinary life? Let me walk you through a hypothetical day to show you how these devotional practices can be woven into the fabric of our lives, not as another set of burdensome tasks, but as a life-giving rhythm of grace.

Morning: You wake up. Before you reach for your phone, you go to your home altar. You light a candle. You take a deep breath. You say a simple prayer: "Good morning, Lord. Good morning, Mary. Good morning, Patrick. Be with me today." You spend a few minutes in silence, or you read a short passage from the life of a saint. You begin your day centred, focused, and in communion.

Midday: You are at work and feeling stressed. A difficult email arrives. An old anger begins to rise. You take a moment. You close your eyes. You whisper a quick "arrow prayer": "Columba, help me!" You take another deep breath. And you respond to the email with grace and patience that are not your own.

Afternoon: You are driving home from work. Instead of listening to the radio, you put on a chant or a hymn. You turn your commute into a mini-pilgrimage. You thank God for the beauty of the sky, for the gift of the day. You talk to your guardian angel, to the saints who are your companions.

Evening: You gather with your family for dinner. It is the feast day of St. Francis. You have a simple meal, and you tell a story about his love for animals. You thank God for the gift of creation and for the example of this joyful saint. After dinner, you spend a few minutes reading a chapter from this book or another book about the saints. You end your day with a prayer of gratitude at your home altar, thanking God and your heavenly family for their presence and their protection throughout the day.

This is not a fantasy. This is a real and achievable way of life. It is a life where every moment—the sacred and the secular, the joyful and the difficult—can become an opportunity for prayer, for communion, for grace. It is a life where our homes become monasteries without walls, and our hearts become temples of the Holy Spirit. It is the life of devotion, the life of the saints. And it is the life to which we are all called.

Practices for This Chapter

1. Create or Refresh Your Home Altar: If you don't have a home altar, create one this week. It can be very simple. If you already have one, take some time to refresh it. Add a new icon, a flower, or an object that is meaningful to you. Make it a place of beauty, a place that draws you into prayer.

2. Celebrate a Feast Day: Look up the liturgical calendar online. Find a saint's feast day that is coming up this week or this month. Plan a simple celebration. Read their story. Eat a special meal. Do an act of service in their honour. Invite the saint to be a guest in your home.

3. Make a Local Pilgrimage: Identify a place in your local area that could be a pilgrimage site for you. It might be a church, a park, a cemetery, or a place of natural beauty. Go there this week with the intention of being a pilgrim. Go in silence. Go with a prayer in your heart. And be open to what God and His saints have to say to you there.

The Goal of Devotion: A Life of Love

It is important to remember that these devotional practices are not the goal in themselves. They are means to an end. And the end is love. The goal is to become a person who is so filled with the love of God that it overflows into love for our neighbour. The goal is to become a saint.

A devotion to the saints that does not lead to a deeper love for the people around us is a sterile and self-indulgent hobby. It is a form of spiritual collecting, of accumulating holy cards and pious practices without allowing them to change our hearts. The saints themselves would be the first to tell us this. They would be horrified to think that we were spending our time honouring them instead of serving the poor, the lonely, the broken—the very people to whom they dedicated their lives.

True devotion to the saints always leads us outward, into the world, in a spirit of love and service. When we spend time with St. Brigid, the great saint of hospitality, we should be moved to open our own homes and our own hearts to the stranger. When we walk with St. Francis, the lover of the poor, we should be moved to simplify our own lives and to share our resources more generously with those in need.

When we pray with St. Thérèse of Lisieux, the master of the "little way," we should be moved to perform our own small, daily duties with great love.

This is the test of the authenticity of our devotional life. Is it making us more loving? Is it making us more compassionate? Is it making us more generous? Is it making us more like Christ? If it is not, then we need to re-examine our motives and our methods. We need to ask the saints to pray for us, that our devotion to them might be purified and become a true path to holiness, a true school of love.

I have had to learn this lesson the hard way. There have been times in my life when I have been so focused on my own spiritual practices, on my prayer times, on my reading, that I have neglected my family's needs. I have been a "holy man" in my study, and a grumpy, impatient husband and father in my living room. And it has often been the saints themselves who have called me out on this.

In the midst of a pious prayer to St. Joseph, the model of fatherhood, I will suddenly be struck with the conviction that I need to play with my children. In the middle of a deep reading of St. Teresa of Calcutta, I will feel a nudge to go and have an honest conversation with my wife. The saints are not interested in our pious self-absorption. They are interested in our transformation. They are interested in our becoming people of love.

So, as you embrace these beautiful and ancient practices, as you build your home altar and celebrate the feast days and go on pilgrimage, remember the goal. The goal is not to become a person who is good at devotions. The goal is to become a person who is good at love. And the saints, our dear friends and companions, are here to help us on that journey, every step of the way.

Chapter 8:

Living in Communion: Daily, Weekly and Seasonal Rhythms

I had a box full of beautiful tools. I had learned to pray with the saints, to sit in contemplative silence, to fast, to create sacred space. I had the theology, the methods, the desire. And I was completely overwhelmed. I would start my week with a burst of spiritual enthusiasm, a zealous commitment to do all the things. I would wake up early for an hour of prayer, fast on Fridays, read the lives of the saints, journal, and do my Lectio Divina. And by Wednesday, I would be exhausted, irritable, and behind on my work. By Friday, I would have given up completely, collapsing on the couch in a heap of spiritual failure, convinced that this kind of deep, intentional life was only for monks in a monastery, not for a busy husband, father, and pastor.

This was my pattern for years: the all-or-nothing cycle of spiritual boom and bust. I would swing from a legalistic, white-knuckled effort to a guilty, defeated apathy. I couldn't find a sustainable rhythm. I was trying to live the life of a saint, but I was doing it with the frantic, anxious energy of a man who was still trying to prove his worth, to earn his salvation, to impress a distant and demanding God.

One day, I was complaining about this to David. "It's impossible," I said. "I can't keep it up. I feel like I'm failing at being a Christian."

David, in his gentle wisdom, asked me a simple question. "Are you trying to be a river, or are you trying to be a tidal wave?"

I didn't understand. "What do you mean?"

"A tidal wave is a huge, dramatic, and destructive event," he said. "It comes in with a roar, and then it's gone, leaving a lot of wreckage behind. A river is a quiet, steady, life-giving force. It flows every day. It's not always dramatic. It just keeps moving, carving a path through the landscape, bringing life wherever it goes. You're trying to live your spiritual life as a series of tidal waves. And you're wondering why you're exhausted, and your life is a mess. God is not calling you to be a tidal wave. He is calling you to be a river."

That image, from the title of my first book, The Ever-Flowing Stream, struck me to the core. I had written about the life of faith as a river, but I wasn't living it. I was still living as if it all depended on me, on my effort, on my ability to generate a tidal wave of spiritual energy. David went on to explain the ancient concept of a "Rule of Life." He told me that the monks in the Celtic monasteries didn't just have a collection of spiritual practices; they had a rhythm, a structure, a Rule that wove those practices into the fabric of their daily lives. A Rule, he explained, is not a set of rigid, oppressive laws. It is a trellis. It is a gentle, supportive structure that allows the vine of our spiritual life to grow, to flourish, to bear fruit.

That conversation changed everything. It was the beginning of my journey out of the boom-and-bust cycle and into a sustainable, life-giving rhythm of communion with God and His saints. It was the journey of learning to live as a river, not a tidal wave. In this chapter, we will explore how to create our own Rule of Life, our own personal trellis. We will learn how to weave the practices we have explored into the daily, weekly, and seasonal rhythms of our lives, not as a burden to be borne, but as a dance to be enjoyed.

The Celtic Sense of Rhythm

The Celtic Christians had a profound sense of rhythm. They lived in a world that was not yet dominated by artificial light and the mechanical clock. Their lives were shaped by the natural rhythms of the world around them: the rising and setting of the sun, the waxing and waning of the moon, the turning of the seasons. And they saw in these natural rhythms a reflection of the spiritual rhythms of God's own life. They understood that our spiritual lives are not meant to be a flat, monotonous line, but a dance, a song, a rhythm of prayer and work, of fasting and feasting, of silence and speech, of solitude and community.

This sense of rhythm is a powerful antidote to the frantic, fragmented, and exhausted pace of modern life. We live in a culture that constantly tells us to do more, be more, and achieve more. We are addicted to the drug of productivity, and our souls are paying the price. We have lost our rhythm. We have forgotten how to rest, how to play, how to be simple.

A Rule of Life is a way of intentionally and prayerfully reclaiming that rhythm. It is a way of creating a gentle, life-giving structure for our days that allows us to stay connected to God and His saints in the midst of our busy lives. It is a way of saying, "The frantic demands of the world will not dictate my life, but by the loving, life-giving rhythms of the kingdom of God."

What is a Rule of Life? A Rule of Life is a personal, prayerfully discerned set of commitments and practices that structure our relationship with God. It is a spiritual trellis. It is a description of how we intend to live our lives, centred on God.

Why have one? A Rule of Life helps us to be intentional about our spiritual growth. It moves us from a life of vague good intentions to a life of concrete, committed practice. It helps us strike a balance among prayer, work, rest, and relationships. It provides a structure that can hold us steady in times of spiritual dryness or emotional turmoil. And it is a powerful tool for resisting the formless, chaotic, and soul-destroying rhythms of our culture.

How do you create one? A Rule of Life is not something you can copy from a book. It is something that you must discern for yourself, in conversation with God, and perhaps with the help of an anam cara or a spiritual director. It should be realistic, flexible, and life-giving. It is not a spiritual straitjacket. It is a dance card. It is a plan for love.

A good Rule of Life will typically include commitments in several key areas:

• **Prayer:** When and how will you pray? (e.g., Daily Office, Centring Prayer, Lectio Divina)

• **Study:** When and how will you study the Scriptures and the lives of the saints?

• **Work:** How will you approach your work as a form of service and worship?

• **Rest and Recreation:** How will you build in time for rest, play, and the enjoyment of God's creation?

• **Relationships:** How will you nurture your relationships with family, friends, and community?

- **Service:** How will you serve the poor and the marginalised?

- **Fasting and Feasting:** What will be your rhythm of fasting and feasting?

In the rest of this chapter, we will explore how to build a Rule of Life around the three great rhythms: the day, the week, and the year.

THE RHYTHM OF THE DAY: THE DAILY OFFICE

The ancient practice of praying at set times throughout the day is called the Daily Office, also known as the Liturgy of the Hours. It is a way of sanctifying time, of weaving prayer into the very fabric of our day. The Celtic monks were masters of this practice. They would gather in their chapels seven times a day to chant the psalms, to hear the Scriptures, and to offer their prayers to God. For them, the day was not just a block of time to be filled with work; it was a sacred journey, a pilgrimage through the hours, and each hour was an opportunity to encounter God.

Most of us cannot pray seven times a day. But we can adopt a simplified version of this ancient practice. We can create a personal Daily Office, a simple rhythm of prayer that punctuates our day and keeps us connected to God and His saints.

Here is a simple model, based on the ancient hours of prayer:

- **Morning Prayer (Lauds):** This is the prayer of the dawn, the prayer of new beginnings. It is a time to offer the day to God, to ask for His blessing and His guidance, and to invite the saints to walk with us through the hours ahead. This might be your most substantial time of prayer. It could include a psalm, a short reading from Scripture or the life of a saint, a time of intercession, and a time of silent contemplation.

You might pray, *"Good morning, Lord. Thank you for the gift of this new day. Be with me in all that I do. Mary, Mother of God; St. Joseph; St. Michael, my guardian angel; St. Patrick; St. Brigid; St. Columba, pray for me. Walk with me today. Help me to love as you loved."*

- **Midday Prayer (None):** This is the prayer of the pause. In the midst of our busy workday, we take a few moments to stop, to breathe, to re-centre ourselves in God. This can be a very short prayer. It might be a simple "arrow prayer," a short, sharp prayer that is shot like an arrow into the heart of God. You might set an alarm on your phone for noon. When it goes off, you stop what you are doing, you close your eyes, and you pray.

"Lord Jesus Christ, Son of God, have mercy on me, a sinner." Or you might call on a saint for help with a particular struggle: "Columba, my brother, I am feeling that old anger rising. Pray for me. Help me to find your peace."

• **Evening Prayer (Vespers):** This is the prayer of the twilight, the prayer of gratitude. It is a time to reflect on the day with gratitude, to thank God for His gifts, and to ask for His forgiveness for our failings. A beautiful practice for this time of day is the Examen, a prayer of review that St. Ignatius of Loyola developed. It has five simple steps:

1. Become aware of God's presence.

2. Review the day with gratitude.

3. Pay attention to your emotions.

4. Choose one feature of the day and pray from it.

5. Look toward tomorrow.

You can do this prayer with the saints as your companions, asking them to help you see your day as God sees it.

• **Night Prayer (Compline):** This is the prayer of the darkness, the prayer of trust and surrender. It is a time to commend our spirits into the hands of God, to ask for His protection through the night, and to rest in the peace of His presence.

This can be a very simple prayer. You might pray the ancient words of the Compline service:

"Protect us, Lord, as we stay awake; watch over us as we sleep, that awake we may watch with Christ, and asleep we may rest in peace."

You might trace the sign of the cross on your forehead. And you might fall asleep whispering the name of Jesus, or the name of a beloved saint.

This simple rhythm of morning, midday, evening, and night prayer can transform our days. It can turn our fragmented, chaotic lives into a sacred pilgrimage, a continuous conversation with God and His saints.

The Rhythm of the Week

Just as we can sanctify our days, we can also sanctify our weeks. We can create a weekly rhythm of prayer and practice that reflects the great rhythm of the Christian story: the rhythm of death and resurrection, of fasting and feasting.

The two great poles of the Christian week are Friday and Sunday.

• **Friday:** This is the day of the Crucifixion. It is a day for sobriety, for remembrance, for penance. It is the traditional day for fasting. On Friday, we remember our own sinfulness and our world's brokenness, and we unite our small sufferings with the great suffering of Christ on the cross. It is a good day to pray the Sorrowful Mysteries of the Rosary, to walk the Stations of the Cross, or to spend some time in quiet prayer before a crucifix. It is a day to remember that we are dust, and to dust we shall return.

• **Sunday:** This is the day of the Resurrection. It is the Lord's Day, the day of new creation. It is a day of joy, of celebration, of feasting. It is the day we gather with our community to celebrate the Eucharist, the great feast of thanksgiving. Sunday is not just a day off from work; it is a holy day, a day set apart for worship, for rest, for family, for the enjoyment of God's good gifts. On Sunday, we remember that we are not just dust; we are beloved children of God, destined for eternal life.

This weekly rhythm of Friday and Sunday, of fasting and feasting, of death and resurrection, is the basic heartbeat of the Christian life. We can build on this basic rhythm by assigning particular themes or saints to the other days of the week. For example:

• **Monday:** A day to pray for our work, for our colleagues, for our mission in the world. A good day to pray with St. Joseph the Worker or St. Patrick.

• **Tuesday:** A day to pray for our struggles, for our spiritual battles, for the grace of courage. A good day to pray with St. Michael the Archangel or St. Columba.

- **Wednesday:** A day of intercession for the world, for the sick, for the poor, for those who are suffering. A good day to pray with Mary, the Mother of God, or St. Teresa of Calcutta.

- **Thursday:** A day to give thanks for the Eucharist and for the gift of the priesthood. A good day to pray with St. John Vianney or St. Thérèse of Lisieux.

- **Saturday:** A day to honour Mary, the Mother of God, and to prepare for the Lord's Day. It is a good day to pray the Rosary and to rest in the quiet expectation of the Resurrection.

This is just an example. You can create your own weekly rhythm, one that is meaningful to you and that fits your own life. The goal is to be intentional, to create a structure that helps you to walk with God and His saints through the days of the week.

The Rhythm of the Year: The Liturgical Seasons

Finally, we come to the great rhythm of the year, the liturgical calendar. As we explored in the last chapter, the liturgical year is a way of living in the story of our salvation. It is a way of journeying with Christ and His saints through the great mysteries of our faith. By aligning our personal spiritual lives with the seasons of the church year, we can enter more deeply into this story and allow it to shape our hearts and our minds.

- **Advent:** This is the season of watchful waiting, of hopeful expectation. It is a time to prepare our hearts for the coming of Christ. We can do this by spending more time in quiet prayer and contemplation, by reading the Old Testament prophecies, and by walking with the great figures of Advent: Isaiah, John the Baptist, and Mary. It is a time to ask, "What am I waiting for? What am I hoping for? How can I make room for Christ to be born anew in my life?"

- **Christmas:** This is the season of feasting and joy, of celebrating the Incarnation. It is a time to marvel at the mystery of God-made-man, to rest in the warmth and the light of the Christ child. We can do this by spending time with family and friends, by singing carols, by enjoying the beauty of the season, and by walking with the shepherds and the magi to the manger in Bethlehem.

• **Lent:** This is the season of repentance, of fasting, of turning back to God. It is a forty-day journey into the desert with Christ, a time to confront our own sinfulness and our need for a Saviour. We can do this by embracing the three great Lenten disciplines: prayer, fasting, and almsgiving. We can walk with the desert fathers and mothers, the great masters of the spiritual life, and ask them to teach us how to confront our demons.

• **Easter:** This is the great fifty-day feast of the Resurrection. It is the season of new life, of joy, of victory. It is a time to celebrate the fact that Christ has conquered sin and death, and that we are a new creation in Him. We can do this by feasting, by singing Alleluia, by spending time in nature, and by walking with Mary Magdalene and the apostles as they encounter the risen Lord.

• **Ordinary Time:** This is the long season that falls between Christmas and Lent, and between Easter and Advent. It is the season of the Spirit, the season of the church, the season of mission. It is the time to live out the mysteries that we have celebrated. It is the time to grow in holiness, to deepen our relationship with God, and to bear fruit in the world. It is the time to walk with the great missionary saints, like Patrick, Columba and Columbanus, and to ask them to help us to be faithful witnesses to the Gospel in our own ordinary lives.

By living in this liturgical rhythm, our lives become a great, unfolding drama. We are no longer just living through another year; we are participating in the great story of salvation. And we are doing it in the company of the whole church, on earth and in heaven.

Grace, Not Perfection

I want to end this chapter with a word of caution, a word that I have had to learn over and over again in my own life. A Rule of Life is a tool, not a weapon. It is a trellis, not a cage. It is a dance card, not a checklist. The goal is not to follow your Rule perfectly. The goal is to love God more perfectly. And you will fail. You will oversleep. You will forget to pray. You will eat a hamburger on a Friday. You will get busy, and your Rule will fall by the wayside. And in that moment, you will be tempted to do what I did for so many years: to give up, to throw in the towel, to collapse in a heap of spiritual failure.

Don't. In that moment, remember the words of the great desert father, Abba Moses: "The most important spiritual practice is to begin again." When you fall, get up. Gently, without judgment, without a long, self-indulgent speech about what a terrible person you are, begin again. Say a quick prayer of sorrow. Ask for God's grace. And take the next small step. This is the path of the saints. They were not people who never fell. They were people who always got back up. They were masters of the art of beginning again.

Your Rule of Life is not meant to be a source of guilt or anxiety. It is meant to be a source of freedom and of joy. It is meant to be a gentle, life-giving rhythm that helps you to stay connected to the God who loves you, and to the great family of saints who are cheering you on. So, hold it lightly. Be flexible. Adjust it as your life changes. And above all, be patient and gentle with yourself. You are a work in progress. And the master sculptor is not finished with you yet.

Practices for This Chapter

1. Draft Your Own Rule of Life: Take some time this week to prayerfully draft a simple Rule of Life. Don't try to be too ambitious. Start small. What are one or two commitments you can make in each of the key areas: prayer, study, work, rest, relationships, service, fasting and feasting? Write it down. Put it somewhere you can see it. And then, try to live it, one day at a time.

2. Establish a Daily Office: Choose one or two of the prayer times from the Daily Office—perhaps Morning and Night Prayer—and commit to practising them every day for one week. See how this simple rhythm begins to shape your days.

3. Live a Liturgical Week: For one week, be intentional about living the rhythm of Friday and Sunday. On Friday, undertake a simple fast (e.g., abstain from meat or a favourite snack). Spend some time in quiet prayer, remembering the Lord's passion. On Sunday, celebrate! Go to church. Have a special meal with your family. Take a nap. Enjoy the gift of the Resurrection.

The Role of Community in a Rule of Life

While a Rule of Life is a personal document, it is not meant to be lived in isolation. The Celtic Christians had a deep understanding of the importance of community. Their monasteries were not just collections of individual hermits; they were vibrant spiritual families, bound together by a shared Rule and a shared love for Christ. The monks prayed together, worked together, ate together, and confessed their sins to one another. They understood that the spiritual life is a team sport. We need each other. We need the encouragement, the accountability, and the wisdom of our brothers and sisters in Christ.

This is why the practice of anam cara, or soul friendship, is so important. As you are discerning and living out your Rule of Life, it is essential to have at least one other person with whom you can be completely honest about your spiritual journey. This is the person you can share your Rule with. This is the person you can confess your failures to. This is the person who can gently call you out when you are being too hard on yourself, or when you are letting yourself off the hook too easily. This is the person who can pray for you and with you.

I would not have been able to find a sustainable rhythm in my own spiritual life without David. He was the one who held my Rule of Life with me. I would meet with him once a month, and we would talk about how it was going. I would tell him where I was struggling, where I was experiencing joy, where I was feeling God's presence, and where I was feeling His absence. And he would listen, and he would ask gentle questions, and he would offer his own wisdom, and he would pray for me. Those conversations were a lifeline. They kept me from giving up. They helped me to see that my struggles were not unique, that my failures were not final, and that God's grace was always available.

If you do not have an anam cara, I encourage you to pray for one. Ask God to bring someone into your life with whom you can share this journey. It might be a friend, a pastor, or a spiritual director. The important thing is that it is someone you can trust, someone who will listen without judgment, and someone who will point you back to Christ.

And as you grow in your own practice, you may be called to be an anam cara for someone else. You may be the one who can offer a listening ear, a word of encouragement, or a prayer of support. This is how the body of Christ works. We bear one another's burdens, and so fulfil the law of Christ (Galatians 6:2). We are a communion of saints, on earth as it is in heaven. And we are all in this together.

A Final Word: The Freedom of the River

I want to return to the image that David gave me, the image of the river. For so many years, I had been trying to live my spiritual life as a series of tidal waves. I was addicted to the drama of the big spiritual experience, the emotional high, the radical commitment. And it was destroying me. It was a life of pride and of despair, of boasting in my successes and of wallowing in my failures. It was a life centred on me.

The journey into a Rule of Life has been a journey into the freedom of the river. A river is not proud. It does not boast. It just flows. It follows the path that has been carved out for it. It is faithful in its slight, daily, unspectacular movement. And in that quiet faithfulness, it brings life to everything it touches. It is a humble and powerful force.

This is the life that God is calling us to. It is a life of quiet, steady, daily faithfulness. It is a life of showing up, of being present, of taking the next small step. It is a life that is not dependent on our feelings or our performance, but on the unshakable, life-giving grace of God. It is a life that is lived in communion with our brothers and sisters on earth and with our great family of saints in heaven.

To live by a Rule is not to be in bondage. It is to be free. It is to be free from the tyranny of our own chaotic impulses, our own shifting moods, our own anxious striving. It is to be free from the soul-destroying rhythms of our culture. It is to be free to love God and to love our neighbour. It is to be free to become the person God created us to be.

So, I invite you to step into the river. I invite you to prayerfully and intentionally create your own Rule of Life, your own spiritual trellis. I invite you to discover the joy and freedom of a life structured by the life-giving rhythms of the kingdom of God. And I invite you to do it all in the good company of the saints, your fellow travellers, your guides, and your friends, who are waiting to welcome you into the great, ever-flowing stream of God's own life and love.

A Practical Example: My Own Rule of Life

To make this more concrete, I want to share with you a version of my own Rule of Life. Please do not see this as a model to be copied. It is the fruit of my own journey, my own struggles, my own discernment. It is what works for me, in this season of my life. I hope that by sharing it, you will be encouraged to create your own, one that is uniquely suited to you.

Daily

- **Morning Prayer (30 minutes):** I begin my day at my home altar. I light a candle. I offer a simple prayer. I read the daily psalm and a short passage from the Gospels. I spend some time in Centring Prayer (20 minutes). I offer my intercessions for my family, my church, and the world. I end by asking for the prayers of my patron saints.

- **Midday Prayer (5 minutes):** I have an alarm on my phone for noon. I stop what I am doing. I pray the Angelus, a beautiful ancient prayer that recalls the Incarnation. I offer a short arrow prayer for whatever is on my heart at that moment.
- **Evening Prayer (15 minutes):** Before dinner, I gather with my family at our home altar. We light the candle. Each of us shares one thing we are grateful for from the day. We pray the Lord's Prayer. We ask for God's blessing on our meal.

- **Night Prayer (10 minutes):** Before I go to sleep, I do a simple Examen of my day. I thank God for His presence. I ask for His forgiveness. I commend my spirit into His hands. I fall asleep praying the Jesus Prayer: "Lord Jesus Christ, Son of God, have mercy on me, a sinner."

Weekly

- **Friday:** I fast from lunch. I spend my lunch hour in quiet prayer, meditating on the Lord's passion. I pray the Sorrowful Mysteries of the Rosary.

- **Saturday:** I spend some time in preparation for Sunday. I read the Scripture readings for the upcoming service. I spend some time in quiet rest and recreation with my family.

- **Sunday:** I attend the Eucharist with my church community. I observe a day of rest from my work. I enjoy a special meal with my family. I take a nap.

Monthly

- I meet with my anam cara, David.

- I go on a half-day local pilgrimage to my oak grove or another place of natural beauty.

- I read a book about a saint or another topic of spiritual reading.

Yearly

- I make a week-long silent retreat at a monastery.

- I observe the seasons of the liturgical year with special prayers, readings, and practices.

This may look like a lot. But it has grown slowly and organically over many years. I did not start here. I started with a simple commitment to five minutes of silent prayer in the morning. And as I was faithful with that small commitment, God gave me the grace and the desire for more. So, I encourage you to start small.

Start with one or two things.

And trust that as you are faithful, the river of God's grace will begin to carve its own life-giving path through your life.

Chapter 9:

St. Patrick: The Courage of the Captive

As I shared in the opening of this book, my first real encounter with a saint as a living companion happened on a day when I felt like a complete and utter fraud. I was leading a Bible study, a respected teacher in my community, a man who was supposed to have all the answers. And a young man named Mark had just shared his story of addiction, of brokenness, of a life that had gone completely off the rails. And in his story, I saw my own. The ghosts of my own violent past, of my own addictions, of my own countless arrests, rose up to mock me. I was a hypocrite, a whitewashed tomb. I fled to the woods, my old sanctuary, but found no peace. The trees seemed to accuse me, the stream seemed to murmur my shame. I was a man drowning.

In desperation, I went home and picked up a book I had bought on a whim, a collection of the lives of the Celtic saints. I opened it at random, and my eyes fell on the story of St. Patrick. I knew the name, of course. I knew the legends of the shamrock and the snakes. But I did not know the man. I began to read his own words, from his Confession, and a sentence leapt off the page and seized my heart: "I was like a stone lying in the deep mud; and He that is mighty came, and in His mercy lifted me up."

I read the words again and again, and tears began to stream down my face. A stone in the deep mud. That was me. That was the perfect description of the shame, the guilt, the self-hatred that was suffocating me. And then the second part of the sentence broke through like the dawn: and He that is mighty came, and in His mercy lifted me up. This was not the story of a plaster saint, a man born with a halo and a harp. This was the story of a man who knew the mud. This was the story of a man who had been rescued. This was my story.

In that moment, Patrick of Ireland ceased to be a historical figure for me. He ceased to be a legend. He became a brother. He became a friend. He became my first anam cara in the communion of saints. He was the one who reached out his hand to me from across the centuries and said, "I know this place. I have been here. And I can tell you, there is a way out. There is a God who is mighty to save."

Patrick was the guide who led me into the vast and beautiful country of the communion of saints. He was the one who taught me that the saints are not distant, perfect beings to be admired, but fellow strugglers, fellow sinners, fellow recipients of an astonishing grace. And he is the one I want to introduce you to first, because his story is the story of the Gospel. It is the story of a God who enters into our brokenness, who meets us in the mud of our lives, and who, in His mercy, lifts us up. In this chapter, we will walk with this great saint. We will learn his story, receive his gifts, and discover how he can become a powerful and compassionate companion on our own journey.

THE STORY OF A SAINT: FROM CAPTIVE TO APOSTLE

To understand Patrick, one must first set aside the legends. Forget the green beer, the leprechauns, the cartoonish figure in a bishop's mitre driving snakes into the sea. The real Patrick is far more interesting, far more complex, and far more human. We are fortunate to know his story from his own hand, through his Confession, one of the most remarkable and personal documents to survive from the ancient world.

He was not Irish. He was born in Roman Britain in the late fourth century, into a relatively privileged and Christian family. His name was Maewyn Succat. His father was a deacon, his grandfather a priest. But by his own admission, his faith was nominal. "I did not know the true God," he writes. He was a typical teenager, comfortable, complacent, and completely unprepared for the tragedy that was about to befall him.

When he was sixteen, his life was shattered. Irish pirates raided his family's estate. He was captured, bound, and taken across the sea to Ireland, where he was sold as a slave. The privileged Roman boy became a shepherd, tending sheep on a cold, lonely mountain in a foreign and hostile land. He was hungry, he was cold, he was utterly alone. He had lost everything: his family, his home, his freedom, his name.

And it was there, in the crucible of his suffering, that he found God. Or rather, that God found him. He writes, "The love of God and his fear grew in me more and more, and the faith grew in me, and the spirit was roused, so that, in a single day, I have said as many as a hundred prayers, and in the night, a like number." The faith that had been a cultural accessory in Britain became his lifeline in Ireland. The God he had not known became his only friend. The empty rituals of his childhood became a desperate, heartfelt conversation. In the mud of his slavery, he found a pearl of great price.

After six years, he had a dream in which a voice told him, "You have fasted well. Soon you will go to your own country." The voice told him that his ship was ready. He obeyed the dream. He walked two hundred miles to the coast, found a ship, and, after a dangerous and challenging journey, eventually returned to his family in Britain. The captive was free. The lost son had returned.

His family was overjoyed. They begged him never to leave them again. And for a time, he was content to stay. He entered the priesthood and began a life of quiet service. But God was not finished with him. He began to have dreams and visions. In one, he saw a man named Victoricus, who had come from Ireland with a great pile of letters.

He gave one to Patrick, which was titled "The Voice of the Irish." And as he read the letter, he seemed to hear the voices of the people from the land of his captivity, crying out to him, "We beg you, holy boy, to come and walk among us once more."

This call was Patrick's second great crisis. It was a call to return to the scene of his trauma, to the land of his slavery, to the people who had brutalised him. It was a call to love his enemies. It was a call that seemed impossible, insane. And he wrestled with it. He resisted it. But the call was relentless. And finally, in an act of incredible courage and obedience, he said yes.

His mission to Ireland was not easy. He faced opposition from the pagan druids, who saw him as a threat to their power. He faced danger from violent chieftains. He faced criticism from his own church authorities in Britain, who regarded him as an uneducated, rustic "stone from the mud." They questioned his motives, his methods, and his authority.

But Patrick persevered. For the next thirty years, he travelled the length and breadth of Ireland, preaching the Gospel, baptising thousands, ordaining priests, and establishing monasteries. He did not come as a conqueror, but as a servant. He did not come to destroy Irish culture, but to baptise it, to find the seeds of the Gospel that were already present in it. He loved the

Irish people with a fierce and tender love. And by the time of his death, he had transformed a nation.

This is the story of St. Patrick. It is the story of a man who was broken and then remade by God. It is the story of a man who was captured and then set free, only to return to the land of his captivity as a missionary of love. It is a story filled with courage, mission, and the astonishing power of forgiveness. And it is a story that has much to teach us today.

The Gifts of St. Patrick

When we walk with a saint, we begin to receive their particular gifts, their unique charisms. They become our mentors, our teachers, our guides in the spiritual life. Patrick has three great gifts to offer us: the courage of the captive, the heart of the missionary, and the grace of forgiveness.

1. The Courage of the Captive: Patrick's courage was not the swaggering bravado of a warrior. It was the quiet, resilient, and deeply humble courage of a man who had been to the bottom and had survived. It was the courage of a man who had lost everything and had discovered that God was enough. This is a very different kind of courage than the one our world usually celebrates. It is not about being fearless; it is about being faithful in the midst of our fear. It is not about being strong; it is about being willing to be weak, vulnerable, and dependent on God.

Patrick's greatest act of courage was not facing down a pagan king. He decided to return to Ireland. It was his willingness to go back to the place of his most profound trauma, to face the memories of his slavery, to love the people who had been his enemies. This is the courage that so many of us need today. We are all held captive by something—by our past, by our fears, by our addictions, by our resentments. And Patrick is the saint who can teach us how to be free.

He is the one who can give us the courage to go back, to face the places of our own brokenness, and to allow God to transform our wounds into sources of healing for ourselves and for others.

When I am afraid, when I am tempted to run from a difficult situation, when I feel the chains of my own past holding me back, I pray to Patrick. I ask him for a portion of his courage. I ask him to remind me that the God who was with him in the lonely fields of Ireland is with me now. And I have found that his companionship gives me the strength to take the next small, frightening step.

2. The Heart of the Missionary: Patrick was one of the greatest missionaries in the history of the church. But his mission was not driven by ambition or by a desire for conquest. It was driven by love. He had fallen in love with God in the crucible of his slavery, and he had fallen in love with the Irish people, the very people who had enslaved him. His heart broke for them. He saw them as "sheep without a shepherd," and he longed for them to know the same saving love that he had experienced.

This is the heart of a true missionary. It is a heart filled with passionate love for God and compassionate love for people. It is a heart that is willing to go to the ends of the earth, to endure hardship, to face opposition, all for the sake of the Gospel. And it is a heart that we are all called to have. We may not be called to go to a foreign country, but we are all called to be missionaries in our own homes, in our own workplaces, in our own communities. We are all called to share the good news of God's love with the people around us, not just with our words, but with our lives.

Patrick is the saint who can help us cultivate this missionary heart. He can teach us how to see the people around us with the eyes of Christ. He can give us a passion for the lost, a courage to speak the truth in love, and a wisdom to connect with the culture around us. When I feel my own heart growing cold, when I am tempted to retreat into the safety of my own holy huddle, I pray with Patrick. I ask him to set my heart on fire with his own missionary love.

3. The Grace of Forgiveness: Perhaps the greatest gift that Patrick has to offer us is the grace of forgiveness. His entire life was a testament to the transformative power of this grace. He forgave the pirates who kidnapped him. He forgave the slave master who bought him. He forgave the people who had held him in bondage. And he returned to them, not with a sword, but with a message of peace. This is the radical, counterintuitive, and world-changing logic of the Gospel. It is the logic of the cross. It is the cruciform life.

And Patrick's forgiveness was not just directed outward. He also had to learn to forgive himself. In his Confession, he is painfully aware of his own sinfulness, his own unworthiness. He calls himself "a sinner, a most simple countryman, the least of all the faithful, and most contemptible to many."

He was haunted by a sin he had committed in his youth, a sin so serious that his enemies used it to try to block his consecration as a bishop. He does not tell us what the sin was. But he tells us that it was a source of deep shame and guilt for him. And yet, he also tells us that he has experienced the overwhelming, liberating grace of God's forgiveness. He knows that he is a stone lifted from the deep mud. And it is this experience of being forgiven that frees him to minister forgiveness to others.

This is a message that we desperately need to hear today. We live in a culture that is characterised by resentment, blame, and unforgiveness. We are held captive by our own wounds and by the wounds we have inflicted on others. And Patrick is the saint who can show us the way to freedom. He is the one who can teach us how to receive the grace of God's forgiveness for our own sins, and how to extend that same grace to those who have hurt us. He is the one who can teach us that forgiveness is not a feeling, but a choice, a decision to release the other person from the debt they owe us, and to release ourselves from the prison of our own bitterness.

Walking with Patrick Today

How can we begin to walk with this great saint? How can we invite him to be our anam cara, our spiritual companion? Here are a few practical ways to begin.

1. Read His Story: The best way to get to know Patrick is to read his own words. His Confession is a short, beautiful, and deeply moving document. Read it not as a history text, but as a letter from a friend. Read it with an open heart. Listen for the ways that his story resonates with your own. What are the places of captivity in your own life? Where have you experienced the mercy of God lifting you from the mud? Where is God calling you to go back, to love, to forgive?

2. Pray His Prayer: There is a beautiful and ancient prayer that is attributed to St. Patrick, known as "St. Patrick's Breastplate." It is a powerful prayer of protection, a prayer that surrounds us with the presence of Christ. You can find many versions of it online. Pray it in the morning as you begin your day. Pray it when you are feeling afraid or discouraged. Let its powerful words become the armour of your soul.

Christ with me, Christ before me, Christ behind me, Christ in me, Christ beneath me, Christ above me, Christ on my right, Christ on my left, Christ when I lie down, Christ when I sit down, Christ when I arise, Christ in the heart of every man who thinks of me, Christ in the mouth of everyone who speaks of me, Christ in every eye that sees me, Christ in every ear that hears me.

3. Walk in His Footsteps: Patrick was a great lover of creation. He found God in the mountains, in the forests, in the fields. You can walk with him by spending time in nature. Go for a walk. Find a quiet place to sit. And listen. Listen for the voice of God in the world around you. As you walk, speak with Patrick. Tell him about your life. Ask for his prayers. You may be surprised at how present he feels.

4. Embrace Your Mission: Patrick can be a powerful companion for us in our own mission, whatever that may be. Are you a parent? A teacher? A doctor? A construction worker? Ask Patrick to help you see your work as a mission field. Ask him to give you a heart of love for the people you serve. Ask him to give you the courage to be a witness to the Gospel in your own small corner of the world.

5. Practice Forgiveness: Is there someone in your life that you need to forgive? Is there a past hurt that you are still holding onto? Bring it to Patrick in prayer. Ask him to help you. He knows how hard it is. He knows the cost of forgiveness. And he knows the freedom that can be found on the other side. He will be a gentle and compassionate guide for you on this difficult but life-giving journey.

Patrick was the first saint who became real to me. He was the one who opened the door for me into the great and glorious reality of the communion of saints. He taught me that the saints are not perfect but are forgiven. They are not distant, but they are near. They are not just examples to be admired, but friends to be loved.

And I know that he can be that for you as well. So, I invite you to get to know this great saint, this apostle to the Irish, this man who was lifted from the mud. I invite you to let him be your brother, your friend, your anam cara. And I promise you, your life will never be the same.

Practices for This Chapter

1. Read the Confession: Find a copy of St. Patrick's Confession online or in a book. Read it slowly, prayerfully, over the course of a week. Keep a journal of the thoughts, feelings, and prayers that arise in you as you read.

2. Pray the Breastplate: For one week, begin each day by praying St. Patrick's Breastplate. Pay attention to how this prayer shapes your day, how it makes you more aware of Christ's presence with you.

3. Take a "Patrick Walk": Go for a walk in a natural setting. As you walk, talk to Patrick. Share your heart with him. Ask for his prayers for your mission, your struggles, and your journey of forgiveness. Listen for his quiet companionship.

The Living Legacy of Patrick

It is a remarkable thing to consider that the faith of an entire nation, a faith that would go on to save civilisation, as the historian Thomas Cahill has argued, was ignited by the courage of one broken man. The legacy of Patrick is not found in the great cathedrals that bear his name, or in the secularised celebrations that have become so common. His true legacy lies in the countless lives transformed by the same Gospel that transformed him.

It is found among the missionaries who, inspired by his example, left the shores of Ireland to bring the light of Christ to a Europe plunged into darkness. It is found in the poets and the scholars and the artists who, nurtured by the faith that he planted, created a culture of extraordinary beauty and learning. And it is found in ordinary people like you and me, who, centuries later, can still find in his story a powerful echo of our own.

I often wonder what Patrick would think of the world today. I think he would be heartbroken by the violence, the injustice, the spiritual emptiness that is so rampant. But I do not think he would be discouraged. He was a man who had seen the worst of humanity, and he had also seen the best of God. He was a man who knew that no darkness is so deep that the light of Christ cannot penetrate it. He was a man who believed in the power of the Gospel to transform even the most hardened hearts.

And I think he would have a particular word for those of us who feel like frauds, like hypocrites, like stones in the deep mud. I think he would look at us with eyes of deep compassion and understanding. And I think he would say, "I know. I have been there. But do not lose hope. The God who lifted me up is with you now. He is mighty to save. And He has a mission for you. He wants to use your brokenness, your story, your life, to bring His light and His love to a world that is dying in the darkness."

This is the living legacy of St. Patrick. It is a legacy of hope, of courage, of mission, of forgiveness. It is a legacy available to us today, not merely as an inspiring story but as a living reality through the communion of saints. Patrick is not just a figure from the past. He is a brother, a friend, a companion for the journey. And he is waiting to walk with you.

The Breastplate: A Deeper Dive

Let's take a closer look at the prayer known as St. Patrick's Breastplate, or the Lorica. While modern scholarship suggests it was likely written in the 8th century by a poet in Patrick's tradition rather than by the saint himself, it perfectly encapsulates the spirit of his faith. It is a powerful expression of the Celtic Christian worldview, a worldview that saw Christ everywhere, in every person, in every circumstance. It is a prayer of radical, all-encompassing trust in Christ's presence and protection.

The prayer begins with a powerful invocation of the Trinity:

I arise today Through a mighty strength, the invocation of the Trinity, Through belief in the Threeness, Through confession of the Oneness of the Creator of creation.

This is not a casual, half-hearted prayer. It is a rising, a girding, a conscious act of stepping into the reality of God's presence. The pray-er is clothing themselves in the power of the Trinity.

This is the foundation of all Celtic spirituality: the deep, abiding reality of the Three-in-One God who is the source of all life and all protection.

The prayer then invokes the power of Christ's life, death, and resurrection. It is a recitation of the creed, not as a dry theological formula, but as a living, active force:

I arise today Through the strength of Christ's birth with His baptism, Through the strength of His crucifixion with His burial, Through the strength of His resurrection with His ascension, Through the strength of His descent for the judgment of doom.

And then comes the invocation of the heavenly host, a powerful reminder that we do not pray alone:

I arise today Through the strength of the love of cherubim, In the obedience of angels, In the service of archangels, In the hope of resurrection to meet with reward, In the prayers of patriarchs, In the predictions of prophets, In the preaching of apostles, In the faith of confessors, In the innocence of holy virgins, In the deeds of righteous men.

This is the communion of saints in action. The one who prays is standing in a great river of faith, a river that flows from the dawn of creation and that carries them forward into the hope of resurrection. A great cloud of witnesses surrounds them, and they are drawing strength from their prayers, their faith, their deeds.

The heart of the prayer, the part that is most often quoted, is the section that we have already seen, the section that surrounds the pray-er with the presence of Christ:

Christ with me, Christ before me, Christ behind me...

This is the essence of the Celtic imagination. Christ is not a distant, heavenly king. He is a constant, intimate companion. He is above, below, within, and without. There is no place where He is not. No part of our lives is outside of His loving, protective presence. To pray this prayer is to consciously and intentionally place ourselves in the forcefield of His love.

It is to say, "I am not alone. I am surrounded. I am safe."

Finally, the prayer ends with a powerful declaration of trust and surrender:

I arise today Through a mighty strength, the invocation of the Trinity...
...Salvation is of the Lord. Salvation is of the Lord. Salvation is of Christ. May Thy Salvation, O Lord, be ever with us. Amen.

In the end, our safety, our salvation, does not depend on our own strength, or even on the strength of our prayer. It depends on the Lord. The Breastplate is not a magic spell. It is an act of faith. It is an act of surrender.

It is a way of saying, "I cannot protect myself. But I know the One who can. And I place my life, my day, my soul, in His hands."

To pray this prayer is to walk in the footsteps of Patrick. It is to know the same radical dependence on God that he knew in the fields of his slavery. It is to know the same intimate companionship with Christ that he knew on his missionary journeys. And it is to know the same unshakable hope in the salvation of the Lord that he knew in the face of every trial and every danger.

It is a prayer for our time, and for eternity.

Patrick's Relevance in a Post-Christian World

It might seem strange to turn to a fifth-century saint for wisdom in our twenty-first-century world. What could this man, who lived in a world so different from our own, possibly have to say to us? I believe he has everything to say to us. In many ways, the world that Patrick was sent to is not so different from the world we find ourselves in today.

He was sent to a pre-Christian culture, a culture that was dominated by paganism, by violence, by a deep spiritual darkness. We are living in a post-Christian culture, a culture that has largely forgotten its Christian roots, a culture that is increasingly hostile to the faith, and a culture that is also marked by a deep spiritual emptiness.

Patrick's mission was not to impose a foreign religion on the Irish people. It was to find the "seeds of the Word," the echoes of the Gospel, that were already present in their culture, and to bring them to fulfilment in Christ. He did not see Irish culture as something to be destroyed, but as something to be baptised. He took their love of nature, their sense of the supernatural, and their deep respect for poetry and story, and showed them how all of these things pointed to the one true God, the God who had revealed Himself in Jesus Christ.

This is a model of missionary engagement that is desperately needed today. We are not called to be culture warriors, to stand on the sidelines and shout about how terrible everything is. We are called to be missionaries, to enter into our culture with the love and the humility of Christ, to find the places of longing, of beauty, of truth, and to show how they are ultimately fulfilled in Him.

Patrick was also a man who knew what it was to be an outsider. He was a Roman in Ireland, a Christian in a pagan land. He was looked down on by the sophisticated churchmen of his own country. He was a man who did not quite fit in anywhere. And yet, it was precisely this outsider status that gave him his power. He was free from the establishment's constraints. He was free to be radical, to be creative, to be led by the Spirit. This is a powerful word for those of us who feel like outsiders in our own culture, in our own churches. Our outsider status is not a liability; it is a gift. It is an opportunity to see things with fresh eyes, to challenge the status quo, to be a prophetic voice in a world deaf to God's voice.

And finally, Patrick was a man who was not afraid of the mud.

He was a man who had been to the bottom and who knew that God's grace was sufficient even there.

He was not a saint who lived in a stained-glass window.

He was a saint who lived in the real world, a world of violence, of suffering, of sin. And he was not afraid to get his hands dirty.

He was not afraid to go to the darkest places, to the most broken people, because he knew that that is where Christ is to be found.

This is the call of the Gospel. It is a call to leave the safety of our own comfortable lives and to go out into the mud of the world, to be with the poor, the marginalised, the forgotten. It is a call to be the hands and the feet of Christ to a world that is hurting. And Patrick is the saint who can give us the courage to answer that call.

In a world that is increasingly fragmented, fearful, and forgetful of God, the story of St. Patrick is a beacon of hope. It is a reminder that one person, filled with the love of God and the courage of the Spirit, can change the world. It is a reminder that our brokenness is not a barrier to God's grace, but a doorway.

And it is a reminder that we are not alone in our mission.

A great cloud of witnesses surrounds us, and at their head is a man who was once a captive, a slave, a stone in the deep mud, and who became an apostle, a saint, a world-changer.

St. Patrick, pray for us.

Chapter 10:

St. Brigid: The Generosity of the Flame

For a long time, my spiritual life was a very masculine affair. It was about struggle, about battle, about discipline. My primary companions were warriors and wrestlers: Patrick, the spiritual soldier who faced down pagan kings; Columba, the fierce poet-monk who wrestled with his own violent temper. I was a man who had come out of a world of fighting, and I understood the spiritual life in those terms. It was a good and necessary stage for me. But it was incomplete.

I discovered this one evening when my wife, Sarah, and I were having one of our periodic and painful conversations about our finances. I was in my usual mode: anxious, controlling, scarcity-minded. I had a spreadsheet for everything. I tracked every penny. I was constantly worried about not having enough. Sarah, who has always been the more generous and trusting one in our relationship, was trying to gently challenge my fear.

"We have enough," she said. "We can afford to be a little more generous. We can have people over for dinner without you having a panic attack about the grocery bill."

I couldn't hear her. All I could hear was the voice of my own fear, a fear that was rooted in the deep poverty and instability of my childhood. I became defensive. I started lecturing her about budgets and savings rates. The conversation escalated, as it always did, and ended with both of us hurt and frustrated. I retreated to my study, fuming, feeling completely misunderstood. I sat at my home altar, intending to complain to Patrick and Columba about how difficult my wife was being. But as I sat there, my eyes fell on a small, simple icon that David had given me, an icon of St. Brigid of Kildare. I didn't know much about her. She seemed gentle, quiet, a bit... tame. Not my usual type.

But for some reason, I picked up the book of Celtic saints and turned to her story. And I began to read. I read the stories of her miraculous, almost reckless generosity. I read about how she gave away her father's prize sword to a leper. I read about how she gave away all her mother's butter, only to have it miraculously replenished. I read about how she prayed for a lake of beer to give to the poor. I read about her monastery at Kildare, a place of radical hospitality, where no one was ever turned away, where the fire of welcome never went out.

And as I read, something in my clenched, fearful heart began to soften. I was looking at a way of being in the world that was the complete opposite of my own. I was a man who was always grasping, always hoarding, always afraid of not having enough. Brigid was a woman who was always giving, always releasing, always trusting in the extravagant, over-the-top abundance of God. Her life was a testament to a truth that my fearful heart could barely comprehend: You can't out-give God.

In that moment, I felt a gentle, humorous, and deeply challenging presence. It was not the warrior energy of Patrick or the fierce intensity of Columba. It was a warm, maternal, and utterly free presence. And I heard a question in the quiet of my heart, a question that was not an accusation, but an invitation: What if you have enough? What if you are safe? What if you could let go, just a little?

I began to weep. They were not the hot, angry tears I was used to. They were tears of release, of relief. I was seeing, for the first time, the prison of my own scarcity mindset. And I was being shown a door. Brigid of Kildare, the gentle saint I had overlooked, became my guide into the frightening and beautiful world of generosity. She became the one who taught me that the spiritual life is not just about fighting; it is also about feasting.

It is not just about discipline; it is also about delight. It is not just about the strength of the warrior; it is also about the generosity of the flame. In this chapter, we will get to know this remarkable woman, this "Mary of the Gael." We will learn her story, we will receive her gifts, and we will discover how she can lead us into a life of greater freedom, generosity, and joy.

The Story of a Saint: The Mary of the Gael

Like Patrick, Brigid's story is wrapped in a thick blanket of legend. And, like Patrick, the legends tell us something true about the saint's heart. While we do not have a personal confession from Brigid's own hand, we have several early biographies, or "Lives," that paint a vivid picture of a woman who was a force of nature, a spiritual powerhouse, and a fountain of extravagant generosity.

She was born in the middle of the fifth century, not long after Patrick began his mission. Her father was a pagan chieftain, her mother a Christian slave. The stories of her childhood are filled with signs of her future holiness. She was said to have been born on the threshold of a house, at the rising of the sun, a symbol of her future role as a bridge between the pagan and Christian worlds, between the old and the new. She was fed on the milk of a white, red-eared cow, a mythical beast from the Celtic Otherworld, a sign that she was a special child, touched by the divine.

From a young age, she showed a remarkable and, to her father, a deeply frustrating generosity. She simply could not stop giving things away. She gave her food to the poor. She gave her mother's butter to the hungry. She gave her father's jewelled sword to a leper so that he could sell it for food. Her father, a man of property and status, was exasperated. He saw her generosity as a form of madness, a threat to the stability of his household. He decided that the best thing to do was to marry her off as quickly as possible.

But Brigid had other plans. She had consecrated her life to Christ. When her father tried to arrange a marriage for her, she prayed that her beauty would be taken away so that no man would want her. According to the legend, one of her eyes swelled up and became disfigured. The suitor was repulsed, and the marriage was called off. Once she was free, her eye was miraculously restored. This story, however strange it may seem to us, is a powerful testament to Brigid's fierce determination to belong to Christ alone.

Finally, her father gave up. He took her to a local bishop to be consecrated as a nun. As she was making her vows, a pillar of fire was said to have shot up from her head to the roof of the church. The bishop, recognising her extraordinary spiritual authority, is said to have accidentally consecrated her as a bishop, a story that, while likely apocryphal, points to the unique and powerful role she would play in the Irish church.

Brigid went on to found a monastery at Kildare, the "Church of the Oak." It was a unique institution, a double monastery for both men and women, with Brigid as the abbess, the leader of the entire community. Kildare became one of the most important spiritual centres in Ireland, a place of learning, of art, and of radical hospitality. It was said that the guest house at Kildare was never empty, and that no one who came seeking food, shelter, or healing was ever turned away. At the heart of the monastery was a perpetual flame, kept burning by the nuns in honour of Christ, the light of the world. This flame became the great symbol of Brigid herself: a source of warmth, of light, and of constant, unwavering welcome.

The stories of her life at Kildare are a cascade of miracles, almost all of them involving her extravagant generosity. She turned water into beer for a group of thirsty lepers. She hung her cloak on a sunbeam. She multiplied food, she healed the sick, she calmed the storms. These stories are not meant to be taken as literal, historical fact. They are icons in words. They are poetic expressions of a deep spiritual truth: that Brigid was a woman so filled with the life of God that the abundance of heaven flowed through her into the world. She was a living, breathing sacrament of God's prodigal, over-the-top, and completely unconditional love.

She was so beloved, so central to the faith of the Irish people, that she became known as the "Mary of the Gael," a second Mary, a mother of the Irish church. She was a figure of immense spiritual power, but also of immense tenderness. She was a bishop and an abbess, but she was also a midwife and a brewer. She was a friend of the poor, a protector of the vulnerable, a woman whose heart was as wide as the sky. And she is a saint who has much to teach us about the flame's generosity.

The Gifts of St. Brigid

If Patrick is the saint of the warrior's courage, Brigid is the saint of the mother's heart. Her gifts are the gifts of warmth, of welcome, of abundance. She has three great gifts to offer us: radical hospitality, prodigal generosity, and a vision of feminine spiritual power.

1. Radical Hospitality: The guest house at Kildare was never empty. This was the core of Brigid's spirituality. For her, hospitality was not just a matter of being polite to visitors. It was a sacred duty, a way of encountering Christ Himself. She lived by the words of the Gospel: "I was a stranger, and you welcomed me" (Matthew 25:35). And she lived by the ancient Celtic tradition of hospitality, which held that to welcome a stranger was to welcome Christ.

This is a radical and counter-cultural message for our world today. We live in a world that is increasingly fearful, suspicious, and closed off. We are taught to fear the stranger, to protect our own, to build walls. Brigid calls us to a different way. She calls us to open our doors, to open our hearts, to see the face of Christ in the face of the stranger, the immigrant, the refugee, the person who is different from us. She calls us to create places of welcome, of safety, of belonging, in our homes, in our churches, in our communities.

When I find myself growing fearful or judgmental, when I am tempted to close my heart to the needs of the world around me, I pray with Brigid. I ask her to give me her wide and welcoming heart. I ask her to help me to see Christ in the person I am most tempted to despise. And I have found that her companionship can melt the ice of my fear and open me up to the surprising joy of welcome.

2. Prodigal Generosity: Brigid could not stop giving things away. She gave away her food, her property, her time, her love. She lived in a state of constant, joy, and seemingly reckless generosity. And the more she gave, the more she seemed to have. Her life was a living parable of the loaves and the fishes, a testament to the miraculous mathematics of God's kingdom, where the more you give away, the more you have to give.

This is the gift that first drew me to Brigid, and it is the gift that I have found most challenging and most liberating. I am a man who is wired for scarcity. I am constantly counting, measuring, worrying. Brigid has been my gentle and persistent guide out of this prison. She has taught me, slowly and patiently, to trust in God's abundance. She has taught me that my security does not lie in my bank account, but in the open hands of a loving Father. She has taught me that the joy is not in the having, but in the giving.

This is not easy. It is a daily struggle. But when I am tempted to hoard my time, my money, my love, I think of Brigid. I think of her giving away her father's sword. I think of her lake of beer. And I ask her for the grace to be a little more like her, a little more free, a little more generous, a little more trusting. And I have found that when I take that small step of generosity, when I open my clenched fist just a little, a surprising joy flows in.

3. Feminine Spiritual Power: Brigid was a woman of immense spiritual authority. She was the leader of a double monastery, a spiritual mother to both men and women. She was a teacher, a healer, a prophetess. She was a woman who was fully alive, fully empowered, fully herself. And in a church and a world that has too often suppressed the gifts of women, her story is a powerful and necessary corrective.

Brigid offers us a vision of a different kind of power, a different kind of leadership. It is not the power of domination, but the power of service. It is not the power of control, but the power of nurture. It is the power of the flame which gives light and warmth to all without diminishing itself. It is the power of the earth which brings forth life in abundance. It is a power that is strong and gentle, fierce and tender, wise and compassionate.

For me, as a man, walking with Brigid has been a journey of integration. She has helped me to honour the feminine in my own soul, the parts of me that are intuitive, relational, nurturing. She has helped me to see that true spiritual maturity is not about being more "manly," but about being more whole. And for the women I know who have a devotion to Brigid, she has been a powerful affirmation of their own spiritual gifts, a source of courage to lead, to teach, to prophesy, to be the strong and beautiful women God created them to be.

Walking with Brigid Today

How can we begin to walk with this "Mary of the Gael"? How can we invite her to be our spiritual mother, our guide into a life of greater generosity and joy? Here are a few practical ways to begin.

1. Make a St. Brigid's Cross: This is a beautiful and ancient tradition. On the eve of her feast day (February 1), people in Ireland would gather fresh rushes and weave them into a distinctive four-armed cross. This cross would then be hung in the home as a symbol of Brigid's protection. You can find instructions for making one online. The act of weaving the cross is a beautiful, meditative practice. And the cross itself is a powerful reminder of Brigid's presence and her promise to protect your home and your family.

2. Practice Hospitality: Take a small, concrete step to be more hospitable. Invite someone over for dinner, especially someone who might be lonely or on the margins—volunteer at a local soup kitchen or homeless shelter. Make your home, your church, your workplace a place of welcome. And as you do, ask Brigid to be with you, to give you her welcoming heart.

3. Practice Generosity: Take a small, concrete step to be more generous. Give away something that you are tempted to hoard. Donate to a charity that serves the poor. Tip a little more extravagantly than you usually would. And as you do, ask Brigid to free you from the fear of scarcity and to fill you with the joy of giving.

4. Pray Her Prayers: There are many beautiful prayers and poems attributed to St. Brigid. Find one that resonates with you and pray it regularly.

One of my favourites is this:

Brigid, you were a woman of peace. You brought harmony where there was conflict, you brought light to the darkness, and you brought hope to the downcast. May the mantle of your peace cover those who are troubled and anxious, and may peace be firmly rooted in our hearts and in our world. In the name of the Father, and of the Son, and of the Holy Spirit. Amen.

The Flame and the Goddess

It is impossible to talk about St. Brigid without talking about the pre-Christian goddess of the same name. The goddess Brigid was one of the most important deities in the Celtic pantheon. She was the goddess of poetry, of healing, and of smithcraft. She was associated with fire, with wells, with the coming of spring. And many of the stories and the symbols that we now associate with St. Brigid were originally associated with her.

For some, this is a problem. It seems to suggest that St. Brigid is not a "real" saint, but just a Christianized version of a pagan goddess. But for the Celtic Christians, this was not a problem at all. It was a sign of the power of the Gospel to baptise, to fulfil, to bring to completion all that was good and true and beautiful in the pre-Christian world. They did not see the goddess as a rival to Christ, but as a signpost, a foreshadowing, a preparation for the Gospel. They believed that Christ was the one true light and that all the smaller lights of the pagan world found their true meaning in Him. And so, they were not afraid to take the stories and the symbols that had been associated with the goddess Brigid and to see them in a new light, the light of Christ.

This is a profound and beautiful model for us today. We do not need to be afraid of the truth and the beauty that can be found outside the walls of the church. We can be confident that all truth, all beauty, all goodness, has its source in God, and finds its ultimate fulfilment in Christ. And we can, like the early Irish Christians, be about the business of baptising, of gathering up all that is good and true and beautiful in our culture and offering it back to God.

Brigid is a saint for our time. In a world that is so often marked by fear, by scarcity, by division, she is a powerful witness to the way of hospitality, of generosity, of unity. She is a reminder that the spiritual life is not just about the hard work of discipline, but also about the joyful play of delight. She is a reminder that God is not a stingy accountant, but an extravagant, prodigal Father who longs to pour out His gifts upon us. And she is a reminder that we are called to be channels of that same extravagant love in the world.

If your spiritual life has been too much in your head, too masculine, too focused on struggle and not enough on joy, I invite you to get to know St. Brigid. Let her be your mother, your friend, your guide. Let her lead you to the warmth of the fire, to the abundance of the feast, to the wide and welcoming heart of God. And you may find that, in her company, your own clenched heart begins to open, and your own life begins to burn with the generosity of the flame.

Practices for This Chapter

1. Make a Brigid's Cross: Find some rushes, reeds, or even paper straws and spend some time this week weaving a St. Brigid's Cross. As you do, pray for her protection over your home and your family. Place the cross in a prominent place as a reminder of her presence.

2. Host a "Brigid's Feast": Invite some people over for a simple meal. It doesn't have to be fancy. The point is the welcome. As you prepare and as you host, ask Brigid to fill your home with her spirit of radical hospitality.

3. Perform an Act of "Prodigal Generosity": Do something this week that feels a little bit reckless, a little bit extravagant. Give away something you are tempted to keep. Make an anonymous donation. Pay for the coffee of the person behind you in line. Do it in secret, and do it with joy, as a way of honouring Brigid and of trusting in the abundance of God.

Brigid and the Earth

Brigid's connection to the natural world is one of her most enduring and appealing characteristics. She is a saint of the earth, a saint of the seasons, a saint who saw the hand of God in the turning of the year and the life of the land. Her feast day, February 1, falls on the ancient Celtic festival of Imbolc, which marked the first stirrings of spring. It was the time when the days began to lengthen, when the ewes came into their milk, when the first green shoots began to push their way through the frozen earth. It was a festival of hope, of new life, of promise.

To walk with Brigid is to become more attentive to the rhythms of the natural world. It is to see the changing of the seasons not just as a meteorological event, but as a spiritual drama. It is to see the hand of God in the budding of the trees, the flowering of the fields, the falling of the leaves. It is to recover a sense of the sacredness of creation, a sense that was so central to the Celtic Christian imagination.

In our own time, when we are so disconnected from the natural world, when we are so often living in a virtual reality of screens and of concrete, Brigid's witness is more important than ever. She calls us to step outside, to put our hands in the dirt, to feel the sun on our faces, to listen to the song of the birds. She calls us to be good stewards of the earth, to care for this precious gift that God has given us. She calls us to see that the world around us is not just a collection of resources to be exploited, but a sacrament of God's presence, a book in which we can read the story of His love.

One of the most beautiful ways to honour Brigid is to create a garden. It doesn't have to be a large or a fancy garden. It can be a few pots on a windowsill, a small patch of earth in a backyard. The act of planting a seed, of watering it, of watching it grow, is a profound spiritual practice. It is an act of hope, of trust, of co-creation with God. And as you tend your garden, you can pray with Brigid. You can ask her to help you cultivate the garden of your own soul, to pull out the weeds of fear and of selfishness, and to plant the seeds of generosity, of hospitality, of joy.

The Challenge of Brigid's Generosity

I do not want to leave you with the impression that walking with Brigid is easy. For those of us who are wired for scarcity, for control, for self-preservation, her way is a profound and daily challenge. Her generosity is not a sentimental, feel-good affair. It is a radical, world-changing, and often frightening way of life. It is a call to a kind of spiritual poverty, a kind of kenosis, a kind of self-emptying.

To give away your father's sword is not a small thing. It is an act of defiance. It is an act of trust. It is an act that has consequences. To live with open hands is to be vulnerable. It is to risk being taken advantage of. It is a risk not having enough. And this is why so few of us are willing to do it.

I still struggle with this every day. I still have to consciously and intentionally choose the way of Brigid over the way of my own fear. I still have to pray for the grace to open my clenched fist. But I have also tasted the joy of it. I have tasted the freedom of letting go. I have seen the miraculous mathematics of God's kingdom at work in my own life. I have seen that when I give, I do not lose, but I gain. I gain a lighter heart. I gain a deeper trust. I gain a wider love.

Brigid is not a comfortable saint. She is a demanding one. She will not let us rest in our comfortable, self-protective little worlds. She will constantly be nudging, challenging, and inviting us to be more generous, more hospitable, and freer. She will be the voice in our hearts that asks, "What if you have enough? What if you are safe? What if you could let go, just a little?" And if we dare to listen to that voice, if we dare to take that small, frightening step of generosity, we will discover a joy that is beyond all measure. All our counting, our wildest dreams.

THE MANTLE OF BRIGID: A CLOAK OF COMPASSION

One of the most famous stories about Brigid tells of how she went to the King of Leinster to ask for land for her monastery. The king, a stingy and hard-hearted man, laughed at her. "I will give you," he said mockingly, "as much land as your cloak will cover." Brigid, undaunted, took off her small cloak and laid it on the ground. And then, miraculously, the cloak began to spread. It spread, and it spread, covering acre after acre of green pastureland, until it had covered a vast and fertile plain. The king, terrified and amazed, fell to his knees and promised to give Brigid whatever she asked. And on that land, she built her great monastery of Kildare.

This story is a beautiful metaphor for the power of Brigid's compassion. Her love, like her cloak, is a thing that expands. It is a thing that takes what is small and makes it large. It is a thing that can cover a multitude of sins, a multitude of sorrows, a multitude of needs. To pray with Brigid is to ask her to spread her mantle of compassion over you, over your family, over your community, over the whole world. It is to ask her to cover our fear with her courage, our scarcity with her abundance, our brokenness with her healing love.

I have a small, hand-woven blanket on my home altar, a blanket that I think of as Brigid's mantle. When I am feeling particularly anxious or afraid, when the world feels like a cold, hostile place, I sometimes take that blanket and wrap it around my shoulders. And as I do, I will pray: "St. Brigid, Mary of the Gael, spread your mantle over me. Cover me with your peace. Warm me with your love. Protect me with your strength." It is a simple, childlike practice. But it is a practice that has brought me great comfort. It is a practice that reminds me that I am not alone, that I am held, that I am loved.

This is a practice that you can adapt for yourself. You can use a blanket, a shawl, or a scarf. The object itself is not magic. It is a reminder. It is a tangible way to experience the spiritual reality of Brigid's compassionate, protective presence. It is a way of saying, "I am a child of God, and I am held in the arms of a loving mother."

BRIGID'S LEGACY: A CHURCH OF WELCOME

What would our churches look like if they were modelled on Brigid's monastery at Kildare?

What if they were places of radical hospitality, where the doors were always open, where the fire of welcome never went out?

What if they were places where the poor, the marginalised, the stranger, were not just tolerated, but celebrated?

What if they were places where the gifts of women were fully honoured, where women were empowered to lead, to teach, to prophesy?

What if they were places of extravagant generosity, where people were not constantly asked for money but continually gave it away?

What if they were places of joy, of feasting, of creativity, of life?

This is the vision that Brigid gives us. It is a vision of a church that is not a fortress, but a hearth. It is a vision of a church that is not a courtroom, but a family. It is a vision of a church that is not a museum for saints, but a hospital for sinners. And it is a vision that is desperately needed today.

So many of our churches are dying, not because the Gospel has lost its power, but because we have lost our nerve. We have become fearful, insular, and self-protective. We have forgotten how to be hospitable. We have forgotten how to be generous. We have forgotten how to be joyful. And so, people are leaving. They are looking for life, and they are not finding it in our churches.

Brigid calls us back to the heart of the Gospel. She calls us back to the way of Jesus, the one who ate with tax collectors and sinners, the one who touched the lepers, the one who welcomed the children, the one who gave His life away for the sake of the world. She calls us to be a church that looks like Him. A church that is a place of welcome, of healing, of hope. A church that is a flame of love in a cold and dark world.

This is not a dream. It is a possibility. And it is a possibility that begins with each one of us.

It begins when we choose to open our hearts, our homes, our wallets.

It begins when we choose to see the face of Christ in the face of the stranger.

It begins when we choose to live not out of our fear, but out of our faith in the extravagant, over-the-top, and completely unconditional love of God.

It begins when we choose to walk with St. Brigid.

Chapter 11:

St. Columba: The Warrior Poet's Transformation

This is the most difficult chapter for me to write. For the past ten chapters, I have been your guide, your anam cara, walking with you into the lives of the saints. But now, we come to the saint who has been my most constant, most challenging, and most intimate companion. We come to the saint who knows the darkest corners of my heart, because they are the same dark corners that he knew in his own. We come to Columba.

I wish I could tell you that my transformation has been a straight line, that the man who was once so full of violence and rage is a distant memory. But that would be a lie. The truth is, the old man is still with me. He is quieter now, most days. But he is still there. And sometimes, he roars.

It happened just a few months ago. It was a stupid thing, a small thing. A disagreement with my teenage son about his grades. It started as a conversation, but his defiance, his disrespect, his pushing of the boundaries, triggered something in me. I felt the old heat rising in my chest, the familiar tightening in my jaw. I felt the surge of adrenaline, the desire to dominate, to win, to crush. My voice got louder. My words became sharper, crueller. I saw the fear in his eyes, and a dark, terrible part of me was glad.

He fled to his room, and I was left standing in the kitchen, shaking, my heart pounding. And then came the shame. A wave of it, so thick and so cold it threatened to drown me. You are a fraud, the old voice whispered. You write books about gentleness and peace, and you are still this monster. You talk about being a man of God, but you are just a thug in a nicer shirt.

Nothing has changed. Nothing will ever change.

I wanted to run. I wanted to drink. I wanted to hit something—the old escapes. But by the grace of God, and after years of practice, I have learned a new way. I stumbled out of the house and went to my small writing shed in the backyard, the place that has become my monastery, my place of exile. I fell into the chair at my home altar, and I did not pray to Patrick for courage, or to Brigid for generosity. I had no room for their virtues. I was in the mud, and I needed someone who knew the mud. I closed my eyes, and I prayed the only prayer I could: Columba. Brother. Help me.

I did not ask him to take the anger away. I knew it was too late for that. I asked him to sit with me in it. I asked him to help me not be consumed by it. I pictured him in my mind, not the serene saint of the stained-glass windows, but the man I had come to know: tall, proud, fierce, his eyes blazing with a holy and a terrible fire. I pictured him sitting next to me in the darkness of my little shed, a silent, powerful presence. He did not offer platitudes. He did not tell me to calm down. He sat with me. And in his presence, I knew that I was not alone. I knew that he understood. He had been here. He had done worse.

And as I sat there, in the quiet companionship of this warrior-saint, the storm in my soul began to subside. The rage did not vanish, but it lost its power over me. The shame was still there, but it was met by a deeper sense of compassion, a compassion that was not my own. It was his. It was Christ's. After a long time, I was able to get up, go back into the house, knock on my son's door, and do the hardest thing in the world: ask for forgiveness.

This is the gift of St. Columba. He is not a saint for the placid or the naturally virtuous. He is the patron saint of the hot-tempered, the proud, the ambitious, the difficult. He is the patron saint of those of us who have a fire in our belly that too often burns out of control. He is the saint who shows us that our greatest wound can become our greatest gift, that our most destructive passion can be transformed into a holy fire, and that the God of grace is not afraid of our darkness. In this chapter, we will walk with this fierce and beautiful saint, this "Dove of the Church." We will learn his story, receive his gifts, and discover how he can be a companion on our own journey of transformation.

The Story of a Saint: The Dove and the Hawk

Columba, or Colum Cille in Gaelic, meaning "Dove of the Church," was born in the early sixth century into the highest echelons of Irish nobility. He was a prince of the ruling Uí Néill clan, a man who could have been High King of Ireland. He was brilliant, charismatic, a gifted poet, a natural leader.

And he had a temper that was the stuff of legend. He was a man of intense passions, of fierce pride, of a deep and sometimes violent sense of justice.

He was, in short, a hawk who had been given the name of a dove.

For the first forty years of his life, the hawk was in the ascendant. He founded several important monasteries in Ireland, including those at Derry and Durrow. He was a powerful and influential figure in the Irish church. But his pride and his temper were a constant source of trouble. The central story of his life, the event that changed everything, revolves around a book.

Columba was a great lover of books, a scholar and a scribe. He visited his old teacher, Finnian of Moville, and while he was there, he secretly, without permission, copied a beautiful new psalter that Finnian had brought from Rome. When Finnian found out, he was furious. He demanded the copy. Columba, in his pride, refused. The case was brought before the High King of Ireland, Diarmait mac Cerbaill, who was Columba's kinsman but also his rival.

The king made a famous judgment: "To every cow her calf, to every book its copy." The copy, he ruled, belonged to Finnian.

Columba was enraged. This was not just about a book. It was about his honour, his rights, his pride. He stormed out of the king's court and rallied his powerful Uí Néill clan. The result was the Battle of Cúl Dreimhne, a bloody and pointless conflict in which, according to the annals, three thousand men were killed. All for the sake of a book.

In the aftermath of the battle, Columba was overwhelmed with remorse. The Irish church held a synod and excommunicated him. Though his excommunication was later lifted, thanks to the intervention of St. Brendan, the guilt of what he had done weighed heavily on him. He sought the counsel of a soul friend, a hermit named St. Molaise. Molaise gave him a sentence, a penance, that was as harsh as his sin was great: he was to leave Ireland, the land that he loved with the passion of a poet, and never return. He was to go into exile, and he was to win as many souls for Christ as had been lost in the battle he had caused.

This was the turning point of Columba's life. This was his peregrinatio pro Christo, his pilgrimage for the sake of Christ. In the year 563, at the age of forty-two, Columba and twelve companions set sail from Ireland in a small coracle. They sailed until they reached a place where they could no longer see the shores of their beloved homeland. They landed on a small, windswept island in the Inner Hebrides of Scotland, an island that would become one of the most important spiritual centres in the history of the world: Iona.

On Iona, the hawk began, slowly and painfully, to be transformed into a dove. The proud prince became a humble abbot. The fierce warrior became a spiritual father. The man who had caused a war over a book spent the rest of his life creating a community that would become a beacon of learning, of art, of mission. From Iona, Columba and his monks launched a mission to the Picts of Scotland, a mission that would eventually lead to the conversion of the entire nation. From Iona, the light of the Gospel would be carried back to a Europe that had been plunged into the darkness of the so-called Dark Ages.

Columba never completely lost his fire. The stories of his life on Iona are still filled with moments of fierce, prophetic anger. But it was an anger that was now consecrated, an anger that was directed not at his own enemies, but at the enemies of God: injustice, oppression, evil. The passion that had once led him to start a war was now channelled into a passionate love for God and for the souls of his people. He became a true Colum Cille, a dove of the church, a man whose life was a testament to the transformative power of God's grace.

He died on Iona in the year 597, surrounded by his monks. His last act was to continue his work of copying the psalms. He laid down his pen in the middle of Psalm 34, at the verse: "They who seek the Lord shall not want for any good thing." He had become the book that he had once been willing to kill for: a living, breathing transcript of the Word of God.

The Gifts of St. Columba

Columba is a challenging and complex saint. He is not for the faint of heart. But for those of us who know the fire of our own passions, the darkness of our own pride, the destructive power of our own anger, he is a priceless companion. He offers us three great gifts: companionship in our struggle with darkness, the hope of transformation, and a vision for the integration of our own warrior-poet souls.

1. Companionship in the Struggle with Darkness: Columba is not a saint who lived on a pedestal. He is a saint who lived in the mud. He knew what it was to be proud, to be angry, to be ambitious, to be consumed by his own ego. He knew what it was to sin, and to sin spectacularly. He knew the devastating consequences of his own actions. And this is why he is such a powerful companion for us. He does not meet us with judgment or with pious platitudes. He meets us with deep, knowing compassion. He can sit with us in the darkness of our own failure, in the shame of our own sin, because he has been there. He knows the way through. He is a living testament to the fact that our darkness does not have the final say. He is a friend to the sinner, a brother to the broken, a guide for the lost.

When I am in the grip of my own anger, my own pride, my own shame, I do not need a saint who will tell me to be better. I need a saint who will say to me, "I know." Columba is that saint. His presence is a silent, powerful reminder that I am not alone, that my struggle is not unique, and that there is hope.

2. The Hope of Transformation: Columba's life is a dramatic story of transformation. The man who began as a proud, violent prince ended as a humble, loving abbot. The man who was exiled for his sin became a missionary who brought the light of Christ to a nation. His life is a powerful witness to the truth that no one is beyond the reach of God's grace. No sin is so great that it cannot be forgiven. No wound is so deep that it cannot be healed. No passion is so destructive that it cannot be consecrated.

Columba shows us that our greatest failures can become the doorways to our deepest transformation. His exile, his greatest sorrow, became the source of his greatest fruitfulness. It was in the loneliness and the hardship of Iona that he was stripped of his pride and his self-reliance. It was there that he learned to depend on God alone. It was there that the Dove finally tamed the hawk.

This is a message of profound hope for those of us who are all too aware of our own failures. We are not defined by our worst moments. We are not trapped in our old patterns. Transformation is possible. And Columba is the saint who can walk with us on that long and difficult road.

3. The Integration of the Warrior-Poet: Columba was a man of contradictions. He was a warrior and a poet. He was a prince and a monk. He was a man of fierce anger and of deep tenderness. And his holiness did not consist in amputating the parts of himself that were difficult or messy. It consisted in offering all of himself, the light and the dark, the hawk and the dove, to be transformed and consecrated by the grace of God.

This is a crucial lesson for those of us who have been taught that the spiritual life is about becoming nice, about suppressing our passions, about being more placid and less intense. Columba shows us a different way. He shows us that God does not want to make us less of who we are, but more. He wants to take our passion, our intensity, our strength, our fire, and to use it for His glory. He wants to turn our warrior hearts into the hearts of spiritual warriors. He wants to turn our poetic souls into the souls of prophets.

Walking with Columba has taught me not to be afraid of my own intensity. It has taught me to see my passion not as a liability, but as a gift. It has taught me to ask not, "How can I get rid of this fire?" but, "How can I offer this fire to God?" It is a lifelong journey, and I fail at it more often than I succeed. But in Columba, I have a companion who understands, a companion who has walked this path before me, a companion who shows me what is possible.

Walking with Columba Today

How can we begin to walk with this fierce and beautiful saint? How can we invite him to be our companion in our struggles with darkness, in our journey of transformation? Here are a few practical ways to begin.

1. Pray the Angry Psalms: Columba loved the psalms. He copied them, he prayed them, he lived in them. And he was not afraid of the so-called "imprecatory" psalms, the psalms of anger, of rage, of crying out for justice. He knew that these psalms were a gift, a way of bringing our most difficult and destructive emotions into the presence of God, where they can be heard, held, and transformed. When you are angry, do not try to suppress it. Do not pretend it is not there. Go to the Psalms. Find a psalm that gives voice to your rage (Psalm 58, Psalm 109, Psalm 137 are good places to start). And pray it with Columba. Pray it out loud. Shout it if you need to. Offer your anger to God, in the company of this saint who knew anger so well. And see what happens.

2. Practice Exile (Peregrinatio): Columba's transformation began with his exile. He had to leave his home, his country, his comfort, his identity, to find his true self in God. We are all called to a kind of peregrinatio. We are called to step out of our comfort zones, to leave behind the familiar, to go to the places that frighten us. This might mean a physical journey, a pilgrimage to a holy place. It might mean a relational journey, a willingness to engage with people who are different from us. It might mean an internal journey, a willingness to face the parts of ourselves that we have been avoiding. Ask Columba to be your guide on your own peregrinatio. Ask him for the courage to leave the shore, to step into the boat, to sail into the unknown. It is in exile that we find our home.

3. Channel Your Passion into Creativity: Columba was a poet. He used his gift for words to praise God, to lament his sins, to tell the story of his faith. He channelled his intense passions into the creative act. This is a powerful practice for those of us who have strong emotions. Find a creative outlet for your passion. Write a poem. Paint a picture. Compose a song. Build something with your hands. Offer your creativity to God as a form of prayer. And ask Columba, the great poet-saint, to inspire you.

Columba is not an easy saint. He will not offer you simple answers or comfortable solutions. He will lead you into the heart of your own darkness. He will challenge you to face your own pride, your own anger, your own capacity for destruction. But he will not leave you there. He will sit with you in the mud. He will walk with you on the long road of repentance. And he will show you the fierce, transformative, and unconditional love of the God who is not afraid of our darkness, the God who can take the most broken and rebellious of hawks and, by His grace, transform them into doves of the church.

If you are a person of intense passions, if you have a fire in your belly that you do not know what to do with, if you are all too aware of the darkness within you, then Columba is the saint for you. He is your brother. He is your friend. He is your anam cara. And he is waiting to walk with you.

Practices for This Chapter

1. Pray an Imprecatory Psalm: This week, when you feel the stirrings of anger, frustration, or injustice, turn to the Book of Psalms. Find a psalm that expresses your feelings (e.g., Psalm 13, 58, or 137). Read it aloud, not as a curse against another person, but as an honest offering of your raw emotion to God. Imagine Columba sitting with you as you pray, understanding and holding your anger in the presence of Christ.

2. Identify Your "Iona": What is the place of "exile" God might be calling you to? It could be a physical place (a retreat centre, a new neighbourhood), a relational challenge (reconciling with an estranged family member), or an internal frontier (facing a long-held fear or addiction). Spend some time in prayer this week, asking Columba for the courage to name your Iona and to take one small step toward it.

3. Create a "Columban" Work: Channel a strong emotion—anger, grief, joy, longing—into a creative act. Write a raw, unfiltered poem. Paint with bold, angry colours. Go for a long, hard run and offer the physical exertion as a prayer. Dedicate this creative act to God, asking Columba to help you consecrate your passion for a holy purpose.

The Scribe and the Sword

It is no accident that the central crisis of Columba's life revolved around a book. For the Celtic Christians, books were not just objects. They were sacred vessels. They were containers of the divine Word. The Gospels were treated with the same reverence as the Eucharist. They were encased in beautiful, jewelled shrines, carried in procession, and their words were believed to have the power to heal, to protect, to bring light into the darkness. To be a scribe, a copier of these sacred texts, was one of the highest callings in the Irish church. It was a form of prayer, a form of meditation, a way of immersing oneself in the very words of God.

Columba was a master scribe. He was a man who loved the beauty of the written word, the feel of the vellum, the smell of the ink. And his love of books was intertwined with his love of God. But in the story of the psalter, his love of the book became disordered. It became a form of pride, of possession, of ego. He wanted the book for himself. He was willing to fight for it, to kill for it. The book, the vessel of the Word of peace, became the occasion for a war. The scribe, the man of the pen, became a man of the sword.

This is a cautionary tale for all of us who love books, who love knowledge, who love theology. It is a reminder that our love of these good things can become a form of idolatry. We can begin to worship the book more than the God the book points to. We can use our knowledge as a weapon, our theology as a way of proving ourselves right and others wrong. We can, like Columba, become so attached to our own understanding of the truth that we are willing to cause division, to wound, to break fellowship for the sake of it.

Columba's journey of repentance was a journey of learning to hold his love of books in a new way. It was a journey of learning to be a scribe not for his own glory, but for the glory of God. It was a journey of learning that the Word of God is not a possession to be hoarded, but a gift to be shared. And it is fitting that his life ended as it began, with a book. But this time, he was not fighting for it. He was giving it away. He was pouring out his life, his last breath, in the service of the Word. The scribe had laid down his sword.

Iona: The Geography of Grace

It is impossible to understand Columba without understanding Iona. The island itself became a character in his story, a partner in his transformation. It is a small place, only three miles long and a mile wide. It is a place of wild and rugged beauty, of granite and of machair, of turquoise water and of white sand. It is a place where the veil between heaven and earth feels very thin.

For Columba, Iona was a place of exile, a place of penance. But it was also a place of profound encounter with God. It was in the harshness of the landscape, in the fury of the storms, in the vastness of the sea, that he met a God who was as wild and as untamed as his own soul. It was in the rhythm of the tides, in the turning of the seasons, in the cry of the seabirds, that he learned a new kind of prayer, a prayer of attentiveness, of listening, of surrender.

Iona became a "thin place," a place where the boundary between the spiritual and the material world is porous. It became a place of pilgrimage, a place where people came from all over Europe to seek God, to find healing, to be in the presence of holiness. And it remains so to this day. To visit Iona is to step into a different kind of time. It is to feel the weight of the centuries of prayer that have soaked into the very soil of the island. It is to walk in the footsteps of Columba and the thousands of saints who have followed him. It is to be reminded that the world is charged with the grandeur of God, and that grace can be found in the most unexpected of places.

But we do not have to go to Iona to find our own thin place. We can find it in our own backyard. We can find it in a city park. We can find it in the silence of our own room. A thin place is any place where we have met God, any place that has become sacred to us through our own experience of His presence. It is a place where we can go to be reminded of who we are and whose we are. It is a place where we can, like Columba, be stripped of our illusions and brought face-to-face with the living God. And it is a place where we can, like him, be transformed.

The Legacy of the Warrior-Poet

Columba's legacy is complex. He is not a simple or an easy saint. But he is a saint for our time. In a world that is so often divided by anger, by pride, by violence, he is a powerful witness to the possibility of transformation. He is a reminder that our passions do not have to destroy us, that they can, by the grace of God, be harnessed for a holy purpose. He is a reminder that our greatest wounds can become the source of our greatest compassion. And he is a reminder that the God we serve is a God of second chances, a God who can turn even the most spectacular failures into a glorious victory.

For those of us who are warriors, who are fighters, who have a fire in our hearts that we do not know what to do with, Columba is our brother. He is the one who can teach us how to be strong without being brutal, how to be passionate without being destructive, how to be angry without sinning. He is the one who can show us how to turn our swords into ploughshares, our battle cries into psalms.

And for those of us who are poets, who are dreamers, who are lovers of beauty, Columba is our master. He is the one who can teach us how to see the world with sacramental eyes, how to find the sacred in the ordinary, how to give voice to the deepest longings of the human heart. He is the one who can show us how to use our gifts not for our own glory, but for the glory of the God who is the source of all beauty.

Columba is the patron saint of the integrated soul. He is the saint who shows us that we do not have to choose between being a warrior and being a poet, between being a person of action and a person of contemplation, between being a leader and being a servant. We can be all of these things. We can be whole. And in our wholeness, we can be a gift to the world.

So let us not be afraid of our own complexity, of our own contradictions, of our own fire. Let us, like Columba, offer all that we are, the light and the dark, the hawk and the dove, to the God who made us, the God who loves us, the God who can, by His grace, make us saints. us saints out of the most unlikely of sinners.

The Prophetic Voice: Speaking Truth to Power

One aspect of Columba's life that is often overlooked is his role as a prophet. He was not just a monk and a missionary; he was a man who spoke truth to power. He was not afraid to confront kings, to challenge injustice, to call the powerful to account. There are many stories of him standing up to the pagan kings of the Picts, of him challenging their druids, of him speaking with a boldness and an authority that came not from his noble birth, but from his anointing by the Holy Spirit.

His exile did not extinguish this prophetic fire. In fact, it was purified. On Iona, he became a spiritual father to kings. Kings would come to him for counsel, for blessing, for a word from the Lord. And he did not flatter them. He did not tell them what they wanted to hear. He spoke the truth, even when it was hard. He called them to be just rulers, to care for the poor, to live in the fear of the Lord.

This is a part of Columba's legacy that is desperately needed today. We live in a world where power is so often abused, where injustice is so often ignored, and where the voices of the poor and the marginalised are so often silenced. And the church is too often silent. We are too often afraid to speak truth to power. We are too often more concerned with being respectable than with being faithful.

Columba calls us to a different way. He calls us to be a prophetic people. He calls us to be a voice for the voiceless. He calls us to be a conscience for our society. He calls us to speak the truth in love, to challenge the powers and principalities of our age, to work for a world that is more just, more compassionate, more in line with the kingdom of God.

This is not an easy calling. It will make us unpopular. It will get us into trouble. But it is the calling of the Gospel. And in Columba, we have a companion who can give us the courage to answer it. When we are afraid to speak, when we are tempted to be silent in the face of injustice, we can pray with Columba. We can ask him for a portion of his prophetic fire. We can ask him for the grace to be a faithful witness, no matter the cost.

The Dove and the Serpent: A Final Contradiction

There is one final story about Columba that I want to share with you. It is a story from Adomnán's Life of Columba, and it is both strange and beautiful. Adomnán tells us that on the day of Columba's death, a white horse, which used to carry the milk-pails from the byre to the monastery, came to the saint as he was sitting, tired and old, in the barn. The horse came and lay its head in Columba's lap, and it began to weep. The monk who was with Columba tried to drive the horse away, but Columba stopped him.

"Let him be," he said. "Let him weep for me. For this creature, who has no reason, has been given by the Creator a knowledge of my departing that has been denied to you."

I love this story. I love it for its tenderness, for its recognition of the deep bond that can exist between humans and animals, for its affirmation of the wisdom of creation. But I also love it for what it says about Columba. The man who was once a hawk, a warrior, a man of violence, had become so gentle, so full of the peace of Christ, that even the animals could sense the holiness in him. The dove had finally, completely, triumphed.

But that is not the end of the story. The name Colum Cille, "Dove of the Church," is not the only name by which Columba was known. In some of the old Irish poems, he is also given the name Crimthann, which means "fox" or "serpent." It is a name that speaks of his cunning, his intelligence, his shrewdness, and his ability to navigate the treacherous political waters of his time. He was a dove, yes. But he was also a serpent.

And in this, he was a true follower of his Master. For Jesus Himself told His disciples, "Behold, I am sending you out as sheep in the midst of wolves, so be wise as serpents and innocent as doves" (Matthew 10:16). This is the paradox of the Christian life. We are called to be innocent, to be gentle, to be harmless. But we are also called to be wise, to be shrewd, to be discerning. We are called to have the heart of a dove and the mind of a serpent.

Columba embodies this paradox. He was a man of deep and simple faith, but he was also a man of great learning and political savvy. He was a man of profound gentleness, but he was also a man of fierce, prophetic fire. He was a man who could weep with a horse and who could stand up to a king. He was a whole and an integrated man. And he is a saint who can teach us how to be the same.

So let us not be afraid of our own contradictions. Let us not be afraid of being both gentle and strong, both wise and straightforward, both a dove and a serpent. Let us, like Columba, offer all that we are to the God who made us, the God who loves us, the God who can, by His grace, make us whole.

And let us, in our wholeness, be a gift to the world, a sign of the kingdom, a testament to the transformative power of the Gospel of Jesus Christ.

Chapter 12:

St. Columbanus, St. Aidan, And St. Kevin: Three More Companions

For the past three chapters, we have walked with three of the great spiritual giants of the Celtic world: Patrick, the courageous apostle; Brigid, the generous hearth-keeper; and Columba, the passionate warrior-poet. For me, these three have been primary companions, a holy trinity of soul friends who have guided me through the most significant passages of my own transformation. Patrick gave me the courage to answer my own call to mission. Brigid taught me to open my clenched fists and my closed heart. And Columba, my fierce brother, has sat with me in the fire of my own anger and shown me the path of repentance.

It would be easy to stop here. It would be easy to think that we have found our companions, our tribe, and that we need no others. But the communion of saints is not a small, exclusive club. It is a vast and glorious family, a great cloud of witnesses with as many different faces as there are stars in the sky. And just as we need different human friends for different seasons of our lives, so too do we need different saints to accompany us on our journey. Sometimes we need a warrior. Sometimes we need a mother. And sometimes, we need a prophet, a pastor, or a hermit.

I learned this lesson a few years ago. I had been reading about the corruption and the injustice in a particular political situation, and I was filled with righteous anger. I prayed with Columba, and his fire met my own. But it was an internal fire, a fire of personal transformation. I felt a call to speak, to act, to do something. And I was afraid. I was afraid of the consequences, of the criticism, of the cost. I needed a different kind of courage, a different kind of fire. I needed a prophet.

Around the same time, a young man in my church, a new believer, was struggling with his faith. I tried to help him. I gave him books. I argued theology with him. I challenged him. And I pushed him away. My passion, my intensity, my desire for him to "get it," came across as judgment. I had the truth, but I had no gentleness. I needed a pastor.

And then there were the days, the long stretches, when the world was too much with me. When the noise of my own life, my own ministry, my own thoughts, was so loud that I could not hear the voice of God. I was busy, I was productive, I was doing "good things." But my soul was starving. I needed a hermit.

In that season of my life, God, in His great mercy, introduced me to three more companions, three more soul friends from the great Celtic family. They were not as famous as Patrick, Brigid, or Columba. Their stories were quieter, their gifts more specific. But they were precisely the saints I needed for that stage of my journey. And I believe they are saints that we all need to know. In this chapter, we will meet them: Columbanus, the fierce prophet; Aidan, the gentle evangelist; and Kevin, the contemplative hermit. They are waiting to walk with us.

St. Columbanus: The Prophetic Fire

If Columba was a hawk transformed into a dove, his younger namesake, Columbanus, was an eagle who remained an eagle throughout his life. He was a man of breathtaking courage, of unyielding integrity, of a fierce and fiery passion for the Gospel that drove him across a continent and brought him into conflict with kings, queens, and even popes. He is not a comfortable saint.

He is a deeply challenging one. And he is a necessary one.

The Story of a Saint: The Restless Pilgrim

Columbanus was born in Leinster, Ireland, around the year 543. He was brilliant, handsome, and tormented by his own passions. As a young man, he was so afraid of the temptations of the flesh that he sought the counsel of a holy woman, a hermitess. She gave him a stark choice: "I, a woman, have chosen the path of Christ. You, a man, are hesitating. Flee, young man, flee!" He fled.

He went to the great monastery of Bangor, under the rule of the strict abbot, St. Comgall. There, for many years, he lived a life of prayer, study, and asceticism. But the fire in his heart could not be contained. He was filled with a restless desire for peregrinatio, for pilgrimage. But his was a different kind of pilgrimage from Columba's. It was not a penance for sin. It was a pure, unadulterated missionary zeal. He wanted to carry the light of the Irish Gospel back to a European continent ravaged by barbarian invasions and fallen into a new kind of paganism.

Around the year 590, at the age of nearly fifty, Columbanus and twelve companions left Bangor and set sail for Gaul, modern-day France. What they found was a corrupt church, a lax clergy, and a decadent, immoral royal court. Columbanus did not try to fit in. He did not compromise. He established a monastery at Luxeuil in the ruins of a Roman fort and implemented the strict, austere, and demanding Rule of Bangor. His community became a beacon of holiness in a dark land. But his prophetic fire soon brought him into conflict with the powers that be.

He clashed with the local bishops over the date of Easter, insisting on the Irish calculation. He clashed with the Frankish king, Theuderic II, and his powerful grandmother, Brunhilda, denouncing their immorality and refusing to bless the king's illegitimate children. He was a thorn in the side of the establishment. And finally, they had enough. In 610, he was arrested and condemned to be deported to Ireland.

But God had other plans. The ship that was to carry him back was driven back to shore by a storm. Columbanus saw it as a sign. He was not done yet. He and his companions made their way through Germany, into Switzerland, and finally over the Alps into Italy. There, in the year 614, he founded his last and greatest monastery, at Bobbio. He died there a year later, a restless pilgrim to the end.

The Gifts of St. Columbanus

Columbanus is a saint for our time. He offers us three crucial gifts: prophetic courage, unyielding integrity, and a restless missionary zeal.

1. Prophetic Courage: Columbanus was not afraid of anyone. He spoke truth to power, even when it cost him everything. He is a powerful companion for those of us who are afraid to speak out against injustice, who are tempted to remain silent in the face of evil. He teaches us that our primary allegiance is not to any earthly power, but to the King of Kings.

2. Unyielding Integrity: Columbanus refused to compromise his faith for the sake of comfort, of acceptance, of power. He lived by a strict and demanding rule, and he called others to the same high standard. In a world that is so often characterised by moral relativism and spiritual laziness, he is a bracing and necessary challenge. He calls us to be Christ's, and not our own.

3. Missionary Zeal: Columbanus was a man on fire with the love of God. He was not content to stay in the comfort of his monastery. He had to go out. He had to share the good news. He is a companion for those of us who have grown comfortable in our faith, who have lost our passion for the lost. He reminds us that the Gospel is not a private possession, but a public proclamation.

Walking with Columbanus Today

Columbanus is not an easy companion. He will not let you rest. He will not let you be comfortable. But if you are feeling a holy discontent, if you are longing for a faith that is more than just a private hobby, if you are ready to be challenged, then Columbanus is the saint for you. Pray with him when you need courage. Read his letters when you need to be reminded of the high calling of the Gospel. And ask him to give you a portion of his prophetic fire.

St. Aidan: The Gentle Evangelist

If Columbanus is the eagle, then Aidan is the dove. If Columbanus is the storm, then Aidan is the gentle rain. He is a saint who shows us a different kind of strength, a different kind of power. He is the saint who teaches us that the most effective evangelism is not about winning arguments, but about winning hearts.

The Story of a Saint: The Apostle of the English

Aidan was a monk from the community of Iona, the monastery founded by St. Columba. He was a man who had been formed in the school of that great and passionate saint. But he had a different temperament. He was quiet, gentle, and humble.

In the year 634, King Oswald of Northumbria, who had been converted to Christianity while in exile on Iona, sent for a missionary to come and evangelise his people. The first monk sent was a man of the Columban school. He was harsh, demanding, and judgmental. And he failed completely. He returned to Iona and reported that the English were too stubborn, too savage, to be converted.

Aidan, who was present at the meeting, spoke up. "Brother," he said, "it seems to me that you were too severe with your unlearned hearers. You should have followed the apostolic practice of giving them first the milk of simpler teaching, and gradually nourished them with the word of God until they were capable of greater perfection."

The abbot and the community were struck by his wisdom, by his "discretion," as the historian Bede puts it. And they knew that they had found their man. Aidan was consecrated as a bishop and sent to Northumbria.

He did not establish his monastery in the royal city of Bamburgh. Instead, he chose the small, tidal island of Lindisfarne, a place that was cut off from the mainland twice a day. It was a place of quiet, of prayer, of retreat. But from this quiet centre, Aidan launched a profoundly incarnational mission. He did not ride a horse, as a bishop was expected to. He walked everywhere. He talked to everyone he met, rich and poor, pagan and Christian. He would stop and speak with them, and if they were not believers, he would invite them to faith. If they were believers, he would strengthen them in their faith and stir them up to good works.

He was a man of great humility and of great poverty. Any money that he was given, he immediately gave away to the poor or used to ransom slaves. He lived a simple, austere life, and he expected the same of his monks. But he was not harsh. He was gentle. He was patient. He was a man who won people to Christ not by the force of his arguments, but by the beauty of his life. King Oswald, who had learned the Irish language during his exile, would often act as Aidan's interpreter as he preached. The king and the saint, working together, brought the light of the Gospel to the people of Northumbria.

The Gifts of St. Aidan

Aidan is a saint for all of us who want to share our faith but are afraid of being pushy, judgmental, or doing more harm than good. He offers us three great gifts: a gentle presence, a compassionate heart, and a discerning spirit.

1. A Gentle Presence: Aidan's power was in his presence. He was simply with people. He walked with them. He talked with them. He listened to them. He did not see them as projects to be converted, but as people to be loved. He is a companion for those of us who need to learn to be more present to the people in our lives, to listen more than we speak, to love more than we judge.

2. A Compassionate Heart: Aidan had a deep and practical love for the poor, the marginalised, the enslaved. He saw the face of Christ in them. He is a companion for those of us whose hearts have grown cold to the suffering of the world. He challenges us to open our eyes, our hands, and our hearts to those in need.

3. A Discerning Spirit: Aidan had the gift of "discretion," the wisdom to know what was needed in a particular situation. He knew when to give milk and when to give solid food. He knew when to challenge and when to encourage. He is a companion for those of us who tend to be one-dimensional in our approach to people, who are either always harsh or always soft. He teaches us to listen to the Holy Spirit, to be attentive to the needs of the person before us, and to respond with wisdom and love.

Walking with Aidan Today

Aidan is a gentle and quiet companion. He will not shout at you. He will walk with you. He will listen to you. If you are longing for a way of sharing your faith that is more about friendship than about argument, more about love than about law, then Aidan is the saint for you. Pray with him before you have a difficult conversation. Ask him to give you his gift of discretion.

And ask him to help you see the face of Christ in every person you meet.

St. Kevin: The Contemplative Hermit

If Columbanus is the eagle and Aidan is the dove, then Kevin is the blackbird. He is a saint who calls us out of the noise and the busyness of the world and into the silence and the stillness of the wilderness. He is a saint who teaches us the language of creation, the prayer of attentiveness, and the joy of simply being with God.

The Story of a Saint: The Man Who Lived in a Tree

Kevin was born in the early sixth century, a contemporary of Columba and Columbanus. He was, like them, of noble birth. But from a young age, he was drawn to a life of solitude and of prayer. He studied in a monastery, but the community life was too noisy for him. He longed for the wilderness.

He went to the beautiful and remote valley of Glendalough, the "valley of the two lakes." There, he lived as a hermit. The stories of his life are filled with a deep and mystical connection to the natural world. It is said that he lived for a time in a hollow tree. It is said that a blackbird laid her eggs in his outstretched hand as he was praying, and that he remained in that position, without moving, until the eggs had hatched and the fledglings had flown away. It is said that an otter would bring him a salmon every day for his food. These are not just charming nature stories. They are stories that point to a deep theological truth: that in Christ, the enmity between humanity and the rest of creation is healed. The saint is the one who has recovered the original harmony of Eden.

Kevin's solitude, however, was not to last. His holiness, his wisdom, his peace, began to attract disciples. They came to him, wanting to learn his way of life. And so, reluctantly, he founded a monastery at Glendalough. It became one of the great spiritual centres of Ireland, a place of learning, of art, of prayer. But Kevin himself remained a hermit at heart. He would often retreat to a small, man-made cave, a "beehive hut," on the side of the upper lake, a place that is still known today as "St. Kevin's Bed." He was a man who lived in two worlds, the world of community and the world of solitude, the world of the abbot and the world of the hermit. He held them together in a creative tension.

The Gifts of St. Kevin

Kevin is a saint for all of us who are drowning in the noise and busyness of modern life and starving for silence, stillness, and a deeper connection with God and the natural world. He offers us three great gifts: a contemplative heart, a deep connection to creation, and the wisdom to balance solitude and community.

1. A Contemplative Heart: Kevin teaches us the importance of silence, of stillness, of simply being in the presence of God. He is a companion for those of us whose prayer life is all words, all thoughts, all activity. He invites us to let go, to be quiet, to listen. He teaches us the prayer of attentiveness, the prayer of the heart.

2. A Deep Connection to Creation: Kevin saw the natural world not as a resource to be exploited, but as a book to be read, a sacrament of God's presence. He is a companion for those of us who have become disconnected from the earth, who live our lives in climate-controlled boxes, who have forgotten that we are creatures of dust and of breath. He invites us to go outside, to pay attention, to see the world with new eyes, to find God in the beauty and the wildness of creation.

3. The Wisdom to Balance Solitude and Community: Kevin lived in the tension between the call to solitude and the call to community. He knew that we needed both. We need times of quiet, of retreat, of being alone with God. And we need times of fellowship, of service, of being together with our brothers and sisters. He is a companion for those of us who tend to go to one extreme or the other, who are either always alone or always with people. He teaches us to find a life-giving rhythm, a holy dance, between the cave and the kitchen, between the wilderness and the city.

Walking with Kevin Today

Kevin is a quiet and gentle companion. He will not shout at you. He will invite you into the silence. He will show you the beauty of the world. If you are feeling overwhelmed, exhausted, disconnected, then Kevin is the saint for you. Pray with him when you need peace. Go for a walk in the woods with him. And ask him to teach you the language of the blackbird, the wisdom of the otter, the stillness of the stone.

Practices for This Chapter

1. Take a Prophetic Stand: In the spirit of Columbanus, identify one issue of injustice in your community or in the world that stirs your heart. This week, take one small, concrete, prophetic action. It could be writing a letter to a politician, joining a peaceful protest, or making a donation to an organisation that is working for change. Before you act, pray with Columbanus for courage and for clarity.

2. Practice Gentle Evangelism: In the spirit of Aidan, choose one person in your life who does not share your faith. This week, make a conscious effort to be a gentle, loving presence to them. Listen to their story. Ask them questions. Pray for them. Do not try to "convert" them. Simply try to love them as Christ loves them. Ask Aidan to give you his gift of discretion.

3. Go on a "Kevin" Retreat: In the spirit of Kevin, schedule a time of silence and of solitude this month. It could be an hour, a morning, a full day. Go to a place of natural beauty. Leave your phone behind. Walk. Sit. Be still. Pay attention to the world around you. Listen for the voice of God in the silence. Ask Kevin to be your guide.

THE TAPESTRY OF COMPANIONSHIP

As we have walked with these three saints, we have seen three very different faces of holiness. Columbanus, the fiery prophet, challenges us to a life of courage and of integrity. Aidan, the gentle pastor, invites us to a life of humility and of compassion. And Kevin, the contemplative hermit, calls us to a life of stillness and of attentiveness. They are a triptych of grace, a threefold cord that is not easily broken.

It can be tempting to choose a favourite, to gravitate toward the saint who is most like us, or the one who offers the gifts that we most desire. And it is good and right to have a primary companion, a patron saint, an anam cara in the communion of saints. But the great gift of the Celtic tradition is its understanding of the body of Christ's diversity. It is not a tradition of "one size fits all" spirituality. It is a tradition that recognises our need for a variety of companions on our journey.

There will be seasons in our lives when we need the prophetic fire of Columbanus. There will be seasons when we need the gentle touch of Aidan. And there will be seasons when we need the quiet stillness of Kevin. The saints are not a pantheon of gods from which we choose our favourite. They are a family, a community, a great cloud of witnesses. And they are all there for us, all the time. We can call on any of them at any time for the specific gift they have to offer.

I have learned this in my own life. There are days when I need to pray with Columbanus before I read the news, asking for the courage to face the injustices of the world without despair. There are days when I need to pray with Aidan before I meet with someone who is struggling, asking for the grace to listen with a compassionate heart. And there are days when I need to pray with Kevin before I go for a walk in the woods, asking for the eyes to see the world as he saw it, as a sacrament of God's presence.

These three saints have become, for me, a kind of spiritual toolkit, a set of companions I can call on for different tasks, challenges, and needs. They have expanded my understanding of what it means to be a saint. They have expanded my understanding of what it means to be a Christian. And they have expanded my heart.

THE DANCE OF THE TRINITY IN THE LIVES OF THE SAINTS

One of the great themes of Celtic Christianity is the Trinity. The Celtic Christians had a deep and vibrant experience of God as Father, Son, and Holy Spirit. They saw the Trinity everywhere: in the three leaves of the shamrock, in the three persons of a family, in the three stages of a human life. And they saw the Trinity reflected in the lives of their saints.

It is not too much of a stretch to see in these three saints—Columbanus, Aidan, and Kevin—a kind of reflection of the three persons of the Trinity. This is not to say that they are divine or to be worshipped. It is simply to say that their lives, their gifts, their personalities, can point us to the different ways that God relates to us.

Columbanus, the fiery prophet, the law-giver, the one who calls us to holiness and to justice, can be seen as a reflection of God the Father. He is the one who establishes the boundaries, who sets the standards, who calls us to account. He is the one who reminds us that God is holy, a God not to be trifled with. And yet, his fire is a fire of love, a fire that is meant to purify us, to make us holy, to draw us into the very life of God.

Aidan, the gentle evangelist, the one who walks with us, who speaks our language, who becomes one of us to win us to Christ, can be seen as a reflection of God the Son. He is the one who embodies the Incarnation. He is the one who shows us the face of God in a human life. He is the one who reminds us that God is a God of humility, of compassion, of self-giving love.

Kevin, the contemplative hermit, the one who draws us into the silence, the one who connects us to the natural world, the one who is the source of all life and all creativity, can be seen as a reflection of God the Holy Spirit. He is the one who breathes life into us. He is the one who opens our eyes to the beauty of the world. He is the one who reminds us that God is a God of mystery, of wonder, of a peace that passes all understanding.

Again, this is not a perfect analogy. It is a poem, not a theological treatise. But it is a way of seeing how the lives of the saints can open up for us a deeper and richer understanding of the God who is Three in One. It is a way of seeing how the communion of saints is not a distraction from God, but a doorway into the very life of the Trinity.

A Family of Friends

As we come to the end of this chapter, and to the end of our introduction to these six great Celtic companions, I hope that you have begun to see them not as historical figures, but as living friends. I hope that you have started to feel a connection to one or more of them, a sense of recognition, of kinship, of belonging.

This is the great gift of the communion of saints. It is the gift of family. It is the gift of knowing that we are not alone. It is the gift of having a great cloud of witnesses who are cheering us on, who are praying for us, who are walking with us every step of the way.

In the chapters to come, we will continue to explore the different ways that we can deepen our relationship with these holy friends. We will look at how we can celebrate their lives in the rhythm of the liturgical year. We will look at how we can share our journey with them within a human community. And we will look at the great hope that they offer us, the hope of a final and glorious reunion in the kingdom of heaven.

But for now, I invite you to rest simply in the company of these new friends. Get to know them. Talk to them. Listen to them. Let them into your life. And see what happens. For I can promise you this: if you open your heart to them, they will open their hearts to you. And your life will never be the same.

The Shadow Side of the Saints

It is important, as we walk with these saints, that we do not romanticise them. They were not perfect. They were human. They had flaws, weaknesses, and a shadow side. And it is often in their shadows, in their struggles, in their failures, that we can find our deepest connection with them.

We have already seen this with Columba. His great sin, the battle he caused, became the doorway to his great repentance and his great fruitfulness. But the other saints had their shadows as well.

Columbanus, for all his prophetic courage, could be harsh, rigid, and unyielding. His strictness, his refusal to compromise, and his fiery temper caused division and conflict wherever he went. He was not an easy man to live with. And for those of us who can be self-righteous, who can be more concerned with being right than with being loving, he is a cautionary tale. He is a reminder that our passion for the truth must always be tempered with love.

Aidan, for all his gentleness, could be seen as politically naive. His refusal to engage with the power structures of his day and his simple, walking-around style of evangelism were beautiful and effective. But it was also, in some ways, a withdrawal from the messy and complex realities of the world. And for those of us who are tempted to retreat into a private, pietistic faith, who are afraid to get our hands dirty in the public square, he is a challenge. He is a reminder that our gentleness must not become an excuse for passivity.

Kevin, for all his contemplative stillness, could be seen as anti-social, as a man who fled from the demands of community. His desire for solitude and his deep connection with the natural world were a great gift. But it was also a temptation. He had to be dragged, reluctantly, into his role as an abbot. And for those of us who are introverts, who are tempted to use our spirituality as a way of avoiding the messy and demanding work of relationships, he is a warning. He is a reminder that our solitude must always be held in tension with our call to community.

To see the saints' shadows is not to disrespect them. It is to see them as whole people. It is to see them as fellow sinners, as fellow strugglers, as fellow pilgrims on the way. And it is to find in their very brokenness a deeper and more authentic hope. For if God could use these flawed and fallible people to do such great things, then surely, He can use us as well.

A Choir of Companions

In the end, the communion of saints is not a collection of individual superstars. It is a choir. It is a great symphony of grace. And every voice is needed. We need the soaring soprano of Brigid's generosity. We need the thundering bass of Columbanus's prophecy. We need the clear, simple melody of Aidan's gentleness. We need the deep, resonant drone of Kevin's contemplation. We need the passionate, complex harmony of Columba's repentance. And we need the steady, courageous baritone of Patrick's faith.

And we need our own voice as well. We are not just listeners to this heavenly music. We are invited to sing along. We are invited to add our own unique and unrepeatable note to the great song of salvation.

So, as we close this chapter, I invite you to listen. Listen to the stories of these saints. Listen to the gifts that they offer. And listen for the one who is calling your name. Who is it that you need to walk with in this season of your life? Is it the prophet, the pastor, or the hermit? Is it the warrior, the mother, or the apostle? Or is it all of them?

Do not be afraid.

They are your family.

They are your friends.

And they are waiting for you with open arms.

Chapter 13:

The Benefits of Walking with the Saints

For the past twelve chapters, we have been on a journey. We have travelled back in time, across the sea to the green shores of Ireland and the windswept islands of Scotland. We have walked with saints and scholars, with prophets and poets, with men and women who were on fire with the love of God. We have listened to their stories, we have learned from their wisdom, and we have begun to see them not as distant historical figures but as living companions, soul friends, anam cara for our own spiritual journey.

But to what end? Why should we bother with these old stories, these ancient lives? In a world that is so focused on the new, the now, the next, why should we turn our attention to the past? What, in the end, are the benefits of walking with the saints? Are they anything more than a collection of inspiring stories, a spiritual hobby for those with a taste for history and a romantic imagination?

I believe they are infinitely more. I believe that cultivating a relationship with the communion of saints is one of the most transformative, most healing, and most hope-filled practices available to the modern Christian. It is a practice that has the power to change everything. It has changed me.

I remember a time, not so long ago, when my spiritual life felt like a lonely and desperate climb up a sheer cliff face in the dark. I was a pastor, a writer, a husband, a father. People surrounded me. But in the deepest places of my soul, I was profoundly alone. The loneliness was more than a feeling; it was a cold, hard reality that shaped my ministry and my life. It made me defensive, territorial. It made me see other pastors not as colleagues but as competitors. It whispered to me that my struggles were unique, that no one could possibly understand the weight of the particular burdens I carried. My prayers felt like they were hitting a brass ceiling. My faith felt like a set of abstract propositions that I had to intellectually assent to and then morally strive, in my own pathetic strength, to live up to. I was exhausted, isolated, and quietly desperate.

It was in that season of spiritual dryness and isolation that God, in His great mercy, opened a door for me. It was not a door I was looking for. It was a low, ancient door, hidden behind the ivy of my own prejudices and preconceptions. It was the door to the communion of saints. It started with a book, a story, a whisper. It started with Patrick, and then Brigid, and then Columba. And as I began to walk with them, to pray with them, to listen to their stories, something began to shift in me. The world began to feel a little less empty. The spiritual life began to feel a little less like a solitary struggle and a little more like a shared journey. I began to realise that I was not alone. I had family. I had friends. I had a great cloud of witnesses who were cheering me on, who were praying for me, who were walking with me every step of the way.

In this chapter, I want to share with you some of the benefits that I have discovered in this practice of walking with the saints. These are not theoretical benefits. These are the real, tangible, life-changing gifts that have come to me as I have opened my heart to this great company of friends. I hope that as you read, you will see that these gifts are not just for me. They are for you, too. They are the inheritance of every person who is in Christ. They are the benefits of belonging to the family of God.

THE GREAT CLOUD OF WITNESSES: A THEOLOGICAL FOUNDATION

The writer of the letter to the Hebrews, after a long chapter recounting the stories of the great heroes of the faith—Abel, Enoch, Noah, Abraham, Sarah, Moses—comes to this stunning conclusion: "Therefore, since we are surrounded by so great a cloud of witnesses, let us also lay aside every weight, and sin which clings so closely, and let us run with endurance the race that is set before us, looking to Jesus, the founder and perfecter of our faith" (Hebrews 12:1-2).

This is the biblical foundation for the communion of saints. The image is powerful. We are not running this race alone. We are running it in a great stadium, and the stands are filled with those who have run the race before us. They are not passive spectators. They are witnesses. The Greek word is martyron, the same word from which we get "martyr." They are those whose lives and deaths bear witness to the truth and the power of the Gospel. They are cheering us on. They are invested in our success. Their lives are a testament to the fact that this race can be run and won.

This is not a metaphor. It is a reality. The Apostle Paul speaks of the church as the "body of Christ" (1 Corinthians 12:27). He does not say it is like a body; he says it is a body. And a body is a single, unified organism. If one part suffers, every part suffers with it; if one part is honoured, every part rejoices with it (1 Corinthians 12:26). Paul does not put a qualifier on this. He does not say, "the parts of the body that are currently alive on earth." The body of Christ is one body, and it transcends time and space. It transcends even death. Death is not a barrier in the body of Christ. It is a doorway. And those who have passed through that doorway are not gone. They are more alive than we are. And they are with us.

This is what we confess every time we say the Apostles' Creed: "I believe in the communion of saints." It is a statement of faith. It is a statement of fact. And it is a statement of profound hope. It means that we are never alone. It means that we have access to a vast reservoir of wisdom, of prayer, of companionship. It means we are part of a story much bigger than our own. It is the story of God's redeeming love, unfolding for centuries and filled with heroes and saints. And we are invited to take our place in that story, to run our leg of the race, surrounded by the love and the prayers of those who have gone before.

BENEFIT 1: THE HEALING OF LONELINESS

The first and perhaps the most profound benefit of walking with the saints is the healing of loneliness. The spiritual life can be a lonely path. People can surround us and still feel like no one understands what we are going through. Our struggles, our doubts, our fears, our longings—they can feel so intensely personal, so unique to us. We can feel like we are the only ones who have ever felt this way.

The saints shatter that illusion. They are the friends who have been there. They are the companions who understand. When I am wrestling with my anger, I can turn to Columba, and I know that he gets it. He has been there. He has done worse. When I am struggling to be generous and to open my heart to the needs of others, I can turn to Brigid, and I know she understands. She has felt the pull of selfishness, and she has found the path of radical hospitality. When I am afraid to answer God's call or to step out in faith, I can turn to Patrick, and I know he knows my fear. He was a captive, a runaway, a man who felt inadequate and unprepared. But he went anyway.

I remember a specific season of ministry that was particularly difficult. A program I had poured my heart into had failed spectacularly. Attendance was low, the volunteers were discouraged, and I was facing criticism from every side. I felt like a complete failure. I remember sitting in my office late one night, surrounded by the debris of my failed project, and the loneliness was a physical weight. I felt like I was the only pastor in the history of the world who had ever messed up so badly. In that moment, I remembered the story of St. John Vianney, the Curé of Ars. He was a simple man, not particularly intelligent or gifted, who was sent to a small, forgotten, and spiritually dead parish in France.

His early years there were marked by failure and opposition. He was ridiculed, ignored, and despised. But he persevered. He prayed. He loved. And over the course of forty years, he transformed that parish into a place of profound spiritual renewal, a place where thousands of people came to find God. As I sat there in my office, I prayed, "St. John Vianney, you know what this feels like. You know the sting of failure. You know the weight of discouragement. Sit with me. Pray for me." And in that moment, the loneliness broke. I was still a failure. The program was still a disaster. But I was not alone. I had a brother who understood.

The saints are our anam cara, our soul friends, in the truest sense of the word. They are the ones who can see into our hearts and understand our deepest struggles, because they have struggled in the same way. They are the ones who can offer us a companionship that is not based on shared interests or life circumstances, but on a shared journey, a shared humanity, a shared love for Christ. They are the friends who will never leave us, who will never forsake us, who will walk with us through the darkest valleys and into the brightest light.

BENEFIT 2: SPIRITUAL MENTORSHIP AND GUIDANCE

We all need mentors in the spiritual life. We need those who are further down the road than we are, those who can offer us wisdom, guidance, and a long view on our immediate problems. In our modern world, such mentors can be hard to find. But in the communion of saints, we have access to the greatest spiritual directors who have ever lived.

The saints are not just our friends. They are our teachers. They are our guides. They have walked the path of holiness and left us a map. Their lives, their writings, their prayers—they are a school of spiritual wisdom. They can teach us how to pray. They can teach us how to love. They can teach us how to fight. They can teach us how to die.

And different saints can offer us different kinds of guidance for different seasons of our lives. When I need to speak truth to power, when I need to find the courage to be a prophetic voice in a world of injustice, I can turn to Columbanus. He will not offer me straightforward answers. He will offer me a fire in my bones and a sword in my hand. When I need to learn how to share my faith with gentleness and with humility, when I need to see the face of Christ in the person in front of me, I can turn to Aidan. He will teach me the power of a quiet presence, of a listening ear, of a compassionate heart. When I need to find God in the silence, in the stillness, in the beauty of the natural world, I can turn to Kevin. He will show me the path of contemplation, the joy of simply being with God.

The saints are a living library of spiritual wisdom. They are a council of elders who are always available to us. We can bring them our questions, our struggles, our decisions. We can ask for their guidance. We can learn from their example. And they will not fail us. They will lead us, with wisdom and with love, into a deeper and more intimate relationship with Christ.

BENEFIT 3: THE POWER OF INTERCESSION

This is perhaps the most misunderstood aspect of the communion of saints. The idea of asking the saints to pray for us can seem strange, even unbiblical, to many modern Christians. It can feel like we are praying to them, as if we are treating them as a kind of junior-varsity god. But that is a profound misunderstanding of what is happening.

When we ask a saint to pray for us, we are not praying to them. We are asking them to pray with us and for us. We are doing exactly what we do when we ask a friend on earth to pray for us. We acknowledge that we are part of a family, that we need each other, and that our prayers are more powerful when they are joined together. The only difference is that the saints are the friends who are in God's very presence. They are the ones who "see him as he is" (1 John 3:2). Their prayers are not hindered by sin, by doubt, by distraction. Their prayers are pure and powerful.

I remember a time when my wife and I were facing a particularly difficult decision. We felt lost, confused, and afraid. We prayed, and we prayed, but we felt like we were getting nowhere. One night, in desperation, I said to my wife, "Let's ask Brigid to pray for us." We had been reading about her life, and we were so moved by her faith, her generosity, her ability to trust God in the midst of impossible circumstances. And so, we prayed a simple prayer: "St. Brigid, our sister in Christ, we are lost. We need wisdom. We need courage. Please, pray for us. Pray with us. Ask our Lord to show us the way."

I cannot tell you that a vision of St. Brigid appeared in our bedroom that night. I cannot tell you that we heard an audible voice from heaven. But I can tell you that something shifted. A peace that was not our own began to settle over our hearts. A clarity that had been eluding us for weeks began to dawn in our minds. The next morning, we knew what we had to do. And we had the peace and the courage to do it.

Was it Brigid who answered our prayer? No. It was God. But I believe with all my heart that our sister Brigid was there with us, that she was adding her powerful prayers to our weak ones, that she was interceding for us before the throne of grace. And I believe that God, in His great love, was pleased to answer the prayer of His family.

To be clear, we do not worship the saints. Worship (latria) is due to God alone. But we do honour them (dulia) in the same way that we honour a beloved grandmother or a respected mentor. We honour them for their faith, for their love, for their witness. And we ask them for their prayers, just as we would ask any member of our family. It is not a distraction from Christ. It is a doorway into a deeper experience of His body, the church.

BENEFIT 4: A DEEPENED AND ENRICHED PRAYER LIFE

Walking with the saints can rescue our prayer life from being dry, abstract, or purely intellectual. The saints give us new ways to pray. They make prayer more relational, more embodied, more creative. They give us a new language for prayer, a new rhythm for prayer, a new imagination for prayer.

When I am angry, I can pray the angry psalms with Columba. When I am feeling overwhelmed by the needs of the world, I can pray the prayer of the "keening woman" with Brigid. When I am longing for a deeper connection with the natural world, I can go for a walk with Kevin and learn to see the world through his eyes. The saints are our prayer partners. They are our prayer teachers. They are our prayer leaders.

They also give us a new focus for our prayers. They teach us to pray not just for our own needs, but for the needs of the world. They teach us to pray for justice, for peace, for the poor, for the lost. They broaden our spiritual horizons. They lift our eyes from our own small concerns and give us a heart for what is on God's heart.

Furthermore, the liturgical calendar, with its cycle of feast days for the saints, provides a new rhythm for our prayer life. Instead of a flat, monotonous landscape, the year becomes a journey through a series of holy seasons, a pilgrimage from one feast to another. Celebrating the feast day of a saint—by reading their story, by praying their prayers, by eating a special meal, by performing an act of service in their honour—is a way of entering into the great story of the church, of aligning our small lives with the great cosmic drama of salvation.

BENEFIT 5: A TANGIBLE CONNECTION TO THE BODY OF CHRIST

In our modern, individualistic culture, it is easy to think of faith as a purely personal matter, a private transaction between God and me. The saints are a powerful antidote to this heresy. They remind us that we are part of a body, a family, a living tradition that stretches back for two thousand years. They connect us to the grand story of the church. They collapse the distance between the past and the present. They make us feel like we belong.

In Book One of this series, we talked about the Celtic idea of "thin places," those places where the veil between heaven and earth seems particularly thin. The communion of saints is a kind of "thin place" in time. It is a place where the past is not past, where the dead are not dead, where the whole family of God is present to us, here and now. To walk with the saints is to step into that thin place. It is to realise that we are not the first to struggle with doubt, to wrestle with sin, to long for God. We are walking a well-trodden path. We are drinking from wells that we did not dig. We are part of a great procession of pilgrims who are all making their way to the same heavenly city. This is a profoundly humbling and a profoundly comforting realisation. It takes the pressure off us to invent our faith from scratch. It gives us a sense of rootedness, of stability, of belonging. It reminds us that we are not alone.

BENEFIT 6: THE GIFT OF A HOLY IMAGINATION

The saints fire our imagination. Their stories—their struggles, their triumphs, their humanity—give us new models for what it means to be a Christian. They show us that holiness is not about a bland, one-size-fits-all perfection. It is about a wild, beautiful, diverse, and sometimes messy adventure of love. It is about offering all of who we are—our passions, our personalities, our gifts, our wounds—to be transformed and consecrated by the grace of God.

The saints show us that there are a thousand different ways to be holy. There is the way of the prophet and the way of the pastor. There is the way of the scholar and the way of the simple peasant. There is the way of the mother and the way of the hermit. There is the way of the warrior and the way of the peacemaker. And all of them are beautiful. All of them are valid. All of them are possible.

I used to be ashamed of my intensity, my passion, my tendency to feel things too deeply. I thought that the spiritual life was about becoming calmer, more placid, more "nice." And then I met Columba. And I realised that God did not want to extinguish my fire.

He wanted to consecrate it.

He wanted to turn my warrior heart into the heart of a spiritual warrior.

He wanted to turn my poetic soul into the soul of a prophet.

Columba gave me a new vision for my own life.

He helped me to see the holiness that was hidden in the very parts of myself that I had been taught to despise.

He gave me the courage to be who I am, to embrace my own unique calling, to live my own story of love.

He gave me the gift of a holy imagination.

The Challenge of the Saints

But the saints are not just a comfort. They are also a challenge. They are not just a warm blanket; they are a sharp sword. They are not just our friends; they are our drill sergeants. They love us too much to leave us as we are. They call us to a higher standard. They challenge our complacency, our compromises, our comfortable sins. They show us what is possible, and in so doing, they expose the poverty of our own spiritual ambitions.

To walk with Columbanus is to be challenged in our comfortable silence in the face of injustice. To walk with Brigid is to be challenged in our stinginess, our closed-fistedness, our carefully guarded resources. To walk with Patrick is to be challenged in our fear, our complacency, and our unwillingness to leave our comfort zones for the sake of the Gospel. The saints afflict the comfortable, and they comfort the afflicted. They do both. And we need both.

If we are only looking for saints who will affirm us, who will make us feel good about ourselves, who are just like us, then we are not looking for saints. We are looking for mascots. The true saints are the ones who get in our face, who call us out, who push us beyond our self-imposed limits. They are the ones who show us that a different kind of life is possible, a life of radical love, of heroic virtue, of complete and utter surrender to God. And they invite us, they challenge us, they dare us to live that life, too.

I remember reading about St. Francis of Assisi and his radical embrace of poverty. I was comfortable. I had a nice house, a reliable car, and a retirement account. I was a good, responsible, middle-class American Christian. And Francis wrecked me. His life was a silent, powerful rebuke to my own. I remember praying, "Francis, you are making me miserable." And I felt his gentle, joyful reply in my heart: "Brother, it is not I who am making you miserable. It is your stuff."

That encounter began a long, slow, and often painful journey for my wife and me, a journey of simplifying our lives, of giving more generously, of detaching our hearts from the love of money and the security of possessions. It was a journey that we would not have taken without the challenging friendship of the poor man from Assisi.

An Invitation to the Feast

These are just a few of the benefits of walking with the saints. There are many more. But I hope that you have begun to see that this is not just a quaint or sentimental practice. It is a powerful and transformative one. It is a doorway into a larger world, a deeper faith, a richer life.

The communion of saints is a great feast, a glorious celebration, a family reunion. And you are invited. You are a member of the family. You have a place at the table. The saints are not looking down on you with judgment. They are looking at you with love. They are cheering you on. They are praying for you. They are waiting for you to take your place.

So, I invite you, my friend, to step into this rich fellowship. I invite you to open your heart to these holy friends. I invite you to begin walking with them, talking with them, listening to them, and letting them into your life. I promise you, if you do, your life will never be the same.

Practices for This Chapter

1. Choose a Patron Saint for the Year: At the beginning of a new year, or a new season of your life, prayerfully choose one saint to be your primary companion for that time. Read their story. Pray with them daily. Ask for their guidance and their intercession. See what God wants to teach you through their friendship.

2. Start a Saints Journal: Keep a journal where you record your experiences of walking with the saints. Write down your prayers to them. Record any insights, any moments of grace, any sense of their presence or their guidance. This will help you to be more attentive to their companionship, and it will become a beautiful record of your journey with them.

3. Pray a Litany of the Saints: A litany is a form of prayer that consists of a series of petitions. The Litany of the Saints is an ancient and beautiful prayer that calls upon the whole company of heaven to pray for us. You can find many versions of it online, or create your own by adding the names of the saints who are most dear to you.

Pray it in a time of need, or as a regular part of your prayer life. Here is a short example:

Lord, have mercy. Lord, have mercy. Christ, have mercy. Christ, have mercy. Lord, have mercy. Lord, have mercy.

Holy Mary, Mother of God, pray for us. St. Patrick, pray for us. St. Brigid, pray for us. St. Columba, pray for us. All holy men and women, pray for us.

4. Share a Story of a Saint with a Friend: The stories of the saints are meant to be shared. They are part of the good news. Choose a story that has touched you, and share it with a friend, a family member, or a small group. You never know how God might use that story to touch their heart and to draw them into the great family of God.

5. Celebrate a Feast Day: Look up the feast day of a saint who is special to you. On that day, please do something to celebrate their life and their friendship. You could read their story, attend a church service, eat a meal that is traditional to their country of origin, or perform an act of service that reflects their particular gifts. For example, on St. Brigid's Day (February 1st), you could bake a loaf of bread and share it with a neighbour, or you could make a donation to a local women's shelter. Let the rhythm of the liturgical year draw you deeper into the life of the communion of saints.

I want to add one more practice, one that is perhaps a bit more personal, a bit more intimate. It is the practice of the "'empty chair.'" It is a practice I have found profoundly helpful in making the communion of saints a more tangible and personal reality in my own life.

Here is what you do.

You find a quiet place, a place where you can be alone and undisturbed.

You set up two chairs, facing each other.

You sit in one of the chairs. The other chair is empty.

You then invite a saint to come and sit with you in that empty chair.

You can choose any saint you like, any holy man or woman who has gone before you in the faith.

You might choose one of the saints we have been walking with in this book.

You might choose a saint from another time or another tradition.

You might even choose a loved one who has died in the faith, a grandparent, a friend, a mentor.

And then, you talk to them.

You open your heart to them.

You tell them what is on your mind, what is weighing on your heart.

You ask them for their wisdom, for their prayers, for their companionship.

You might read a story from their life.

You might pray one of their prayers.

You might sit in silence with them, enjoying their presence.

I know, it sounds strange. It might feel strange. But I can tell you from my own experience that it can be a powerful and beautiful practice. It is a way of engaging your imagination, your body, and your emotions in the reality of the communion of saints. It is a way of making that abstract doctrine a living, breathing reality. It is a way of saying, with your whole being, "I am not alone. I have a family. I have friends. And they are with me."

I remember one time when I was feeling particularly overwhelmed by the demands of ministry. I was tired, discouraged, and on the verge of burnout. I set up two chairs in my study. I sat in one, and I invited St. Columba to sit in the other. I told him about my struggles, my frustrations, my sense of failure. I told him that I felt like I was pouring myself out for nothing, that my work was making no difference. I asked him, "How did you do it? How did you keep going, year after year, in the face of so much opposition, so much hardship, so much disappointment?"

I did not hear an audible voice.

But as I sat there in the silence, I felt his presence, a sense of his solidarity. And a thought came into my mind, an idea that was not my own. It was a thought full of his fiery, passionate, yet deeply compassionate spirit.

The thought was this: "You are not called to be successful. You are called to be faithful. You are not called to build a great kingdom. You are called to plant a small seed. And you are not responsible for the harvest. That is God's business. Your business is to be faithful to the work that He has given you to do, to love the people that He has given you to love, and to trust Him with the results."

In that moment, something broke open in me. A burden that I had been carrying for years was lifted. I was set free from the tyranny of results, from the need to be a "successful" pastor. I was set free simply to be a faithful one. It was a moment of profound grace, a moment of deep and lasting healing. And it came to me in the quiet of my study, in the company of a long-dead Irish saint, in the practice of the empty chair.

So, I invite you to try it. I invite you to be brave, to be a little bit foolish, and to see what God might have for you in this simple, powerful practice. You might be surprised at who shows up. You might be surprised at what they have to say.

Deeper into the Communion: More Stories from the Journey

As I reflect on the benefits I've shared, I realise that each one is not just a concept, but a lived reality, a collection of moments where heaven has touched earth in my own life. The saints are not abstract principles; they are persons, and our relationship with them is personal. Allow me to share a few more stories, a few more snapshots from my journey with these holy friends, in the hope that they will encourage you to embark on your own.

The Saint of Second Chances

I once had a friendship that was broken, seemingly beyond repair. It was a classic story of misunderstanding, pride, and words spoken in anger. For years, a painful silence existed between this person I had once considered a brother and me. I prayed about it, of course, but my prayers were tinged with self-righteousness and a desire for vindication. I wanted him to be the one to apologise, to admit he was wrong. The bitterness was a stone in my heart.

Around that time, I was reading about St. Columba, and specifically about his later years. As we've discussed, Columba was a man of fierce passions, and his early life was marked by a prideful and contentious spirit that led to a bloody battle and his subsequent exile from Ireland. But the Columba of his later years on Iona was a different man. He was a man who had been humbled, a man who had learned the painful lesson of his own sinfulness, a man who had become a channel of God's peace and reconciliation. He was a man who understood the need for a second chance.

One evening, I was praying, and I felt a nudge to invite Columba into my prayer for this broken friendship. I pictured him in my mind's eye, not as the young, fiery prince, but as the old, weathered abbot of Iona, his face etched with the lines of repentance and grace. I said, "Columba, you know what it's like to mess up, to let your pride and your anger get the best of you. You know the pain of a broken relationship. Pray for me. Pray for my friend. Help me to let go of my pride and to be the first to extend a hand of peace."

It wasn't a magic wand. The bitterness didn't disappear overnight. But something began to soften in me. The story of Columba's own repentance gave me a new perspective on my own. It helped me see my part in the conflict, my need for grace. It gave me the courage to write a letter, not of accusation, but of confession and of hope. It was a simple letter, but it was one of the hardest things I have ever written. And it opened a door. The friendship was not restored overnight, but a conversation began. A process of healing was set in motion. And I do not doubt that my hot-headed, grace-filled friend, St. Columba, was there in the midst of it, interceding for two prideful men in need of a second chance.

The Saint of the Ordinary

Not all encounters with the saints are dramatic. In fact, most of them are quiet, subtle, and woven into the fabric of our ordinary lives. For me, one of the most constant and comforting companions has been St. Thérèse of Lisieux, the young French Carmelite nun who died of tuberculosis at the age of 24. Thérèse is not a saint of grand gestures or epic adventures. She is a saint of the "Little Way," the path of doing small things with great love.

There are seasons in my life, as I'm sure there are in yours, that feel anything but epic. They are seasons of diapers and dishes, of deadlines and carpools, of a thousand small, repetitive, and often thankless tasks. In these seasons, it is easy to feel that our lives are insignificant, that we are not doing anything "great" for God. It is easy to fall into the trap of believing that holiness is for other people, for the missionaries, the martyrs, the mystics.

Thérèse is the patron saint of the rest of us. She is the patron saint of the ordinary, the hidden, the mundane. Her life was a testament to the truth that holiness is not about what we do, but about the love with which we do it. She found God not in grand ecstasies, but in the patient endurance of community life, in the cheerful completion of her assigned chores, in the simple, childlike trust she placed in the merciful love of God her Father.

I have a small picture of Thérèse on my desk. And there are countless times when, in the midst of a frustrating day, I have looked at her smiling face and have been reminded of her "Little Way." I remember one afternoon when I was trying to write, but I was constantly interrupted by my young children. I was growing more and more frustrated, my heart filled with a very un-pastoral irritation. I looked at Thérèse, and I remembered her story of being splashed with dirty water by another nun in the laundry. Instead of reacting with anger, she saw it as an opportunity to offer a small sacrifice of love to Jesus. It was a simple story, but it was a profound one. And it was a gentle rebuke to my own selfish irritation.

I took a deep breath. I looked at my children, not as interruptions to my "important" work, but as the work itself. I saw their needs not as a distraction, but as an invitation to love. I didn't suddenly become a perfect, patient father. But in that moment, Thérèse helped me to see my ordinary, frustrating day with new eyes. She helped me to see it as a field of love, a place where I could, in some small way, offer my own "little way" to God. Walking with the saints does not remove us from the messiness of our ordinary lives. It plunges us more deeply into it. But it does so with a new sense of purpose, a new understanding of perspective, and a new sense of hope. It helps us to see that our small, hidden lives are not insignificant.

They are the very places where God wants to meet us.

They are the very places where Holiness is to be found.

A Final Word: Your Own Journey

I have shared with you my stories, my friends, my journey into the beautiful and life-giving reality of the communion of saints. But my story is not the most important one. The most important story is the one that you are living, the one that you are writing with your own life.

My hope, my prayer, is that this chapter has been an invitation. It is an invitation to open a door that you may have thought was locked. It is an invitation to explore a room in the great house of the Christian faith that you may have never entered. It is an invitation to a feast, a friendship, a family.

I do not know which saints will become your companions. I do not know what stories will capture your imagination. I do not know what benefits you will discover on your own journey. But I know this: if you accept the invitation, if you take the first step, you will not be disappointed. You will find that you are not alone. You will find that you have a great cloud of witnesses who are cheering you on. And you will find that your own life, your own story, is a part of a much larger and more beautiful story than you ever dared to imagine.

So, go in peace, my friend.

And may the saints of God walk with you, every step of the way.

Bibliography for Walking with the Saints

This bibliography provides a curated list of resources for further study on Celtic Christianity, the lives of the saints featured in this book, and the theological concept of the communion of saints. It is organised into three sections: General Works on Celtic Christianity, Lives of the Saints, and Theological Works on the Communion of Saints.

GENERAL WORKS ON CELTIC CHRISTIANITY

- Bradley, Ian. Celtic Christianity: Making Myths and Chasing Dreams. Edinburgh University Press, 2019.

- Cunliffe, Barry. The Ancient Celts. Oxford University Press, 2018.

- De Waal, Esther. The Celtic Way of Prayer: The Recovery of the Religious Imagination. Morehouse Publishing, 2003.

- Hughes, Kathleen. The Church in Early Irish Society. Wipf and Stock Publishers, 2005.

- Joyce, Timothy J. Celtic Christianity: A Sacred Tradition, a Vision of Hope. Orbis Books, 1998.

- Meek, Donald E. "Modern Celtic Christianity." In Celticism, edited by Terence Brown, 143-157. Rodopi, 1996.

- O'Donohue, John. Anam Cara: A Book of Celtic Wisdom. HarperCollins, 1997.

- O'Loughlin, Thomas. Discovering Saint Patrick. Orbis Books, 2005.

- Ryan, John. Irish Monasticism: Origins and Early Development. Four Courts Press, 1992.

• Simpson, Ray. Celtic Christianity: Deep Roots for a Modern Faith. Grove Books, 2019.

• Stokes, George Thomas. Ireland and the Celtic Church: A History of Ireland from St. Patrick to the English Conquest in 1172. Society for Promoting Christian Knowledge, 1886.

LIVES OF THE SAINTS

St. Patrick

• Freeman, Philip. St. Patrick of Ireland: A Biography. Simon & Schuster, 2004.

• Saint Patrick. The Confession of Saint Patrick. Translated by John Skinner. Image Books, 1998.

St. Brigid of Kildare

• Connolly, Séan, and Jean-Michel Picard, trans. Cogitosus: Life of Saint Brigit. Journal of the Royal Society of Antiquaries of Ireland 117 (1987): 5-27.

• Ritari, Katja. Saints and Sinners in Early Christian Ireland: Moral Theology in the Lives of Saints Brigit and Columba. Brepols, 2009.

St. Columba of Iona

• Adomnán of Iona. Life of St. Columba. Translated by Richard Sharpe. Penguin Classics, 1995.

• Broun, Dauvit. Adomnán's 'Life of Columba'. In Spes Scotorum, Hope of Scots: Saint Columba, Iona and Scotland, edited by Dauvit Broun and Thomas Owen Clancy, 81-106. T&T Clark, 1999.

Other Celtic Saints

• Bieler, Ludwig, ed. and trans. The Irish Penitentials. The Dublin Institute for Advanced Studies, 1963. (Contains rules attributed to Columbanus)

- Walker, G.S.M., ed. and trans. Sancti Columbani Opera. The Dublin Institute for Advanced Studies, 1957. (The works of St. Columbanus)

THEOLOGICAL WORKS ON THE COMMUNION OF SAINTS

- Balthasar, Hans Urs von. "The Communion of Saints." Communio: International Catholic Review 15, no. 2 (1988): 132-149.

- Johnson, Elizabeth A. Friends of God and Prophets: A Feminist Theological Reading of the Communion of Saints. Continuum, 1998.

- Ratzinger, Joseph (Pope Benedict XVI). Introduction to Christianity. Translated by J.R. Foster. Ignatius Press, 2004. (See especially the section on the Apostles' Creed).

- Sproul, R.C. The Communion of Saints. Ligonier Ministries, 2008.

- Walford, Stephen. Communion of Saints: A Treasury of Patristic and Medieval Exegesis. Angelico Press, 2019.

www.ingramcontent.com/pod-product-compliance
Lightning Source LLC
Chambersburg PA
CBHW020930090426
42736CB00010B/1097